Real Relationships

Using Real Colors® to Build Personal Connections

Written by Dr. Dan Johnson
for

National Curriculum & Training Institute, Inc.

For further information on **Real Colors**® or NCTI please contact:

National Curriculum & Training Institute®, Inc.
P.O. Box 60905 • Phoenix, Arizona 85082-0905

(800) 622-1644 • E-Mail: info@ncti.org

Or visit our Web site at www.realcolors.org

Printed in China.

ISBN 0-9754153-2-8

Contents

Introduction

This guide is designed to help you apply **Real Colors**® concepts to your daily relationships with other people. By this time you have probably attended a **Real Colors** workshop where you have been introduced to the power of temperament in helping you understand yourself and others. Although it is not absolutely necessary, you will also find it helpful to have read *The Real Colors*® *Homeowner's Guide.* The guide provides useful tips on developing a deeper understanding of your own personality – where your Blue, Gold, Green, and Orange characteristics come from, what they look like in action, and how you can balance the reality of who you are with the demands of everyday life.

The Real Relationships Table moves to the next level by answering the question, "How can I use **Real Colors** to improve my relationships with other people?" It is not a dating or marriage manual, but we will explore those relationships. It is not a set of tips for making friends, but it will help you improve friendships.

In this guide I use a table analogy to explore the dynamic balance that can be created between two people so that they understand and respect one another's strengths and liabilities. When you feel comfortable enough with another person to invite them into your home, you can ask them to share your table, to share conversation, and to explore one another's hopes and

Introduction

dreams. Opening yourself to this type of personal connection carries with it both opportunities and obstacles. It takes a willingness to risk, to trust one another enough to share the personal details that can only be shared from inside your Color home.

In the first chapter you will review the Colors by considering what individuals bring to the table – your personality "stuff." You will look at your Color "stuff" in terms of how it can either promote or impede your own personal growth. In chapter two you will learn ways to share your personality stuff with other human beings as well as how to appreciate their stuff. In chapter three you will learn how to promote and sustain a positive balance between your stuff and their stuff – monitoring and growing a personal relationship. In chapter four you will learn how two people can use Real Colors to create a positive attitude toward one another and toward life in general. In the fifth chapter you will learn a key Real Colors caution: manage your environment, not your relationships. And in the final chapter you will explore the nuances of Real Colors in various stages of intimacy.

There are no magic bullets for ensuring meaningful and lasting relationships, but there are numerous lenses through which you can develop a clearer picture of potentially positive relationships in the world around you. Real Colors provides such a lens. Let's look at how that lens can help you develop and sustain meaningful relationships with other human beings.

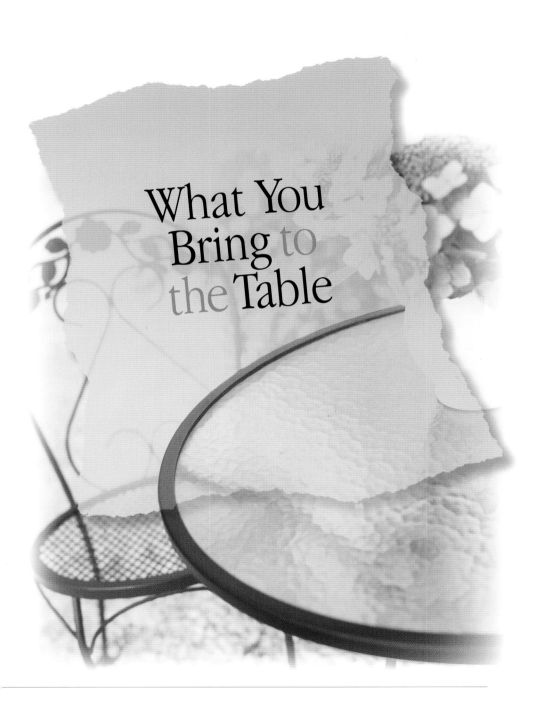

What You Bring to the Table

What You Bring to the Table

In the *Real Colors Homeowner's Guide* (2004) we used a homeowner's analogy to emphasize the role that the colors can play in your life. The Real Colors System is like a home for your personality. When you learn to apply the colors in a balanced way, you feel safe enough to invite others into your world and, in turn, feel more relaxed in their world. But what happens as you begin to form relationships with others?

Grace is an easygoing person who sees life as a search for people who enjoy the things she enjoys. She spends most of her day in a job that requires order and discipline and allows little time to deal with people on a personal basis. She lives in an apartment house of young, upwardly mobile professionals who are either on the go or partying around the pool. Her

Mrs. Carter

friends at work go to a bar once or twice a week to have a cocktail and dance. Grace usually avoids both party scenes but often finds herself either eating a pizza alone while watching a video or spending time with Mrs. Carter in apartment 403 who reminds Grace of her grandmother who lives three states away.

Jack lives in Grace's apartment complex but fits into this young singles scene. He has a technology job that gives him immediate feedback and plenty of opportunities to win the boss's attention. Jack usually plans the staff's weekly parties that include dancing and an occasional volleyball tournament. He drives a sports car and knows everybody in the apartment complex. No one at work or in the complex would think of having a party without inviting Jack. Mrs. Carter loves him and only pretends to be offended by his risqué flirting. She smiles and shakes her head when she sees Jack dancing with a different young lady at each week's party. She says she doesn't know when Jack will grow up, but Grace isn't certain whether Mrs. Carter wishes Jack would grow up or that she were young enough to dance with him at the pool parties.

Grace and Jack sometimes talk briefly as they pass one another in the hall or when they are coming and going from Mrs. Carter's apartment. Both seem to be slightly enchanted with the other, but neither seems willing to take the first step. What do Grace and Jack find interesting in each other? What keeps them from acting on those interests? Relationships between two people can be either frustrating or rewarding — usually a little bit of both. They make people stronger and at the same time more vulnerable. They are at times difficult to initiate and almost impossible to predict. But while there is no absolute way of predicting all the nuances of a relationship, there are certain things that you can do to make them more rewarding.

The first of these is to know what you bring to the relationship table. But before we set this table, let's take a moment to review the aspects of the house in which this table will be placed. The following paragraphs are meant to be a summary of key Real Colors concepts. For a more in-depth review you may want to refer to the *Homeowner's Guide*.

A Homeowner's Review

Figure 1.1. illustrates the Real Colors as a floor plan for a four-room house.

The Basic Real Colors® Floor Plan
Figure 1.1

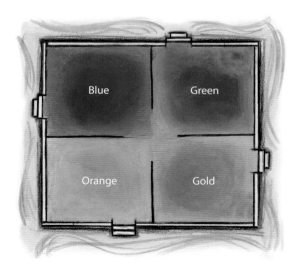

What You Bring to the Table

Each room in this house has its own exterior entrance. But as you know, you will tend to use one of these four entrances more than the other three, and once inside the house, you will spend more time in some rooms than in others. You can learn to use different entrances from time to time and to feel comfortable in any room, but when you become so accustomed to entering your house through the same door and spending most of your time in one or two rooms, you limit your ability to use the other rooms effectively. Remember, "A liability is the result of carrying a strength too far."

You may develop a strength to such an extent that you impede other aspects of your personality. You get so busy functioning in your preferred color that you forget to develop other colors. At times you may not feel appreciated for who you are – when parents, family, friends, and work responsibilities prevent you from spending enough time in your preferred room or from moving from room to room in the order that feels most comfortable to you.

However, it is difficult, if not impossible, to change your color order. And it is generally counterproductive to focus on your liabilities. A negative approach generally will not get you the balance you are seeking (or that others would prefer). It may even decrease your ability to excel in your preferred color.

Let's suppose that Grace and Jack, mentioned earlier, want to get to know one another. Grace wonders if she should try to be more like Jack? What will happen if she starts to attend the parties at the apartment complex or if Jack invites her to a party with his office friends? Will Jack find her dull? Will she like his friends or find them pushy like the "jocks" who seldom invited her to parties in high school – the ones, in fact, that Grace had vowed she would always avoid? Or should Grace invite Jack to the theatre? He would surely not find it inappropriate for a girl to ask a guy out, but would he go to the theatre – with Grace? Would he find the theatre interesting or just go to please her? Would he feel uncomfortable with her theatre friends or worse, would he embarrass her in front of them?

Should Jack try to be more like Grace? Should he try to be more refined and less boisterous? Should he explain that he loves his sports car but has never had a speeding ticket – that he learned from an accident years ago to take high speeds to a racetrack? Should he tell her that he finds the theatre interesting even if he really likes comedies more than drama? What would happen if he told her that Mrs. Carter pays him to walk her dog or that he actually saw Mrs. Carter as a conduit to get to know another gorgeous red-head – Grace?

Grace and Jack could benefit from a brief review of their Real Colors and a reminder to focus on their strengths. The fundamental message of the Real Colors System is that the first step in getting along with others is getting along with yourself – understanding and accepting who you are. Victor Frankl (1959) described this balance as a "search for meaning." Such meaning comes from being your own color while still doing all of the colors.

What You Bring to the Table

The balance between personal fulfillment and getting along with others is seldom perfect and never static. The people and events of your world affect the range and intensity of your colors. And that range and intensity shifts constantly. If family and friends support you in good times and bad and encourage you to build on your strengths, your success may become an avenue to develop other positive skills and attitudes. On the other hand, if they constantly chide you for your failures, you may withdraw or wait for them to tell you what to think and do.

You can gain a better understanding of how your attitudes toward your Color order are formed by looking at how your order compares to the rest of the world and, more specifically, to your family, friends, etc. Keirsey's research (1998) places Color percentages among the general population as follows:

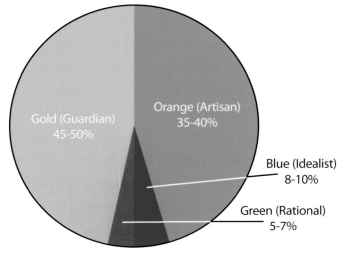

(See www.keirsey.com for more current statistics.)

What You Bring to the Table

Golds and Oranges find meaning in concrete, real world experiences. They focus on the real world through their senses of sight, hearing, smell, touch, and taste. Oranges are tacticians who value facts and events as potential opportunities to discover and enjoy. Golds tend to be logistical, valuing facts and events in terms of how they fit predefined parameters.

Blues and Greens search for meaning in a more abstract world – in connections that lie beyond facts and events. They function more intuitively focusing on the connections between and among people and events. Blues focus on the spiritual or emotional impact of facts and events. Greens focus on logical connections and underlying principles. Among these intuitive, big-picture folks Blues outnumber Greens.

While both Golds and Oranges focus initially on concrete events and experiences, they process those experiences in different ways. Likewise, Blues and Greens both focus on connections among events and experiences but they process those connections from significantly different perspectives. However, a more significant factor lies in the imbalance between concretes and abstracts. Oranges and Golds combined outnumber Blues and Greens combined by more than two to one. It is obviously easier for Golds or Oranges to find people who share their views. Since there are fewer Blues and Greens in the world, the abstract individuals find themselves having to fit in. On the other hand, their unique way of looking at the world can create a special demand for their abilities and services. Figure 1.2 illustrates the significance of this imbalance.

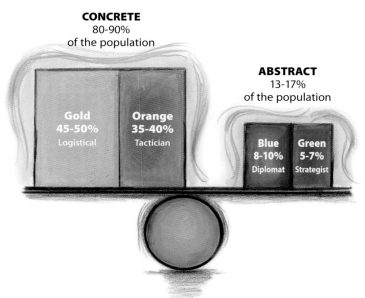

CONCRETE
80-90%
of the population

ABSTRACT
13-17%
of the population

Gold
45-50%
Logistical

Orange
35-40%
Tactician

Blue
8-10%
Diplomat

Green
5-7%
Strategist

The Concrete-Abstract Imbalance
Figure 1.2

It is difficult not to stereotype other Colors based on your experiences. How you are appreciated or unappreciated has a tremendous influence on your actions. Again, I like to think of the four colors in terms of what I have called the 4-P's (Johnson, 2005). Figure 1.3 lists each of these P's by Color along with a question designed to guide your thinking as you apply the Color to real life situations.

The 4-P's
Figure 1.3

Color	4-P's	4-P Questions
Blue	Purpose	What makes this important?
Gold	Parameters	What are the rules of the game?
Green	Principles	How will I make this work?
Orange	Priorities	Will it make a difference?

Blue represents your need to understand how things connect to a higher *purpose*. Gold represents your attempt to manage or control the daily activities of life according to accepted *parameters*. Green represents your need to understand how things connect in terms of logical strategies or underlying *principles*. Orange represents your attempt to seize the moment, to experience as many aspects of life as possible in the time allotted – acting on your *priorities*.

Every human being is born with the capability of functioning in each of the four Colors. In fact, it is impossible to function in life without addressing all of them. By thinking of the Colors in terms of the 4-P's, you can begin to see how you need each. You can refer to the *Real Colors Homeowner's Guide* to gain a better understanding of the following questions.

What You Bring to the Table

1. *How much stuff (the way I look at the world) have I collected in each room of my Colors home?*

2. *Where did my Color stuff come from?*

3. *How often and how effectively do I use my Color stuff?*

4. *How comfortable do I feel when I use each Color?*

5. *How have past decisions regarding Colors affected movement throughout my Colors home?*

You can also use the Guide to review the clues (clues are not absolutes) that people give you about their Colors through their words and actions.

Listening for Color Clues
Figure 1.4

When a Blue is pleased…	*When a Blue is agitated…*
What would you like to do today?	Why can't people be more understanding about…?
When a Gold is pleased…	*When a Gold is agitated…*
Let's get our work finished or we can't…	Why can't people be more responsible when it comes to…?
When a Green is pleased…	*When a Green is agitated…*
I think we ought to look at this situation more closely…	If people only took the time to think about…
When an Orange is pleased…	*When an Orange is agitated…*
Hey, I know! Let's…	I wish someone would do something; anything would be better than…

What You Bring to the Table

Now let's shift our attention from how these individual characteristics interact with one another to how they form a balance within a relationship. Use the following analogy to think about your place at the Colors table.

Setting the Relationship Table

A common way of getting to know people is to invite them to share a meal at your home (although I will admit that this custom has been lost somewhat in today's fast-paced society). Your comfort level with them and with yourself often determines whether you want to have a cookout or a sit down meal. Before considering what they bring to the table, you may want

Figure 1.5

to ask yourself what you bring — what assets you have to offer them. Think first about the room in which you want to place your table?

Since you are hosting this meal, the first consideration should be where you will feel most comfortable. Use Figure 1.5 to think about where you will feel most comfortable serving a meal and carrying on a conversation.

What You Bring to the Table

Placing Your Relationship Table

Let's assume that you have chosen to place your table in the Blue room, a bright room filled with art and soft music with flowers and artifacts from around the world. But what Color is your guest? The following chart suggests some dinner plans to suit each Color.

Ambiance and Cuisine
Figure 1.6

Blue	Gold
Ambiance: Already perfect. Provide a before dinner period for conversation. *Cuisine:* Unique appetizer from another culture, colorful entrée, light dessert, and a time after dinner to continue the conversation.	*Ambiance:* Prepare normal appetizers served in the living room. Begin the meal on time. *Cuisine:* Pleasant but basic (unique sauce for a beef Wellington). Water and perhaps wine with a loaf of French bread. Light dessert served shortly after the meal. Adjourn to the living room for coffee and conversation.

Green	
Ambiance: Prepare a unique appetizer that can serve as a conversation piece. *Cuisine:* Prepare a unique entrée in a unique way. Relate every other part of the meal, including dessert, to your central theme. After dinner adjourn for coffee and conversation in the gallery.	

	Orange
	Ambiance: Serve a funky appetizer on the patio. *Cuisine:* Prepare a simple entrée with a zesty sauce. Keep it simple so that you can adjourn to the game room for dessert and a few hands of cards.

What You Bring to the Table

Ambiance is important, but it means different things to each Color. Blues generally prefer a quiet setting where they can talk and get to know one another. They appreciate a meal that demonstrates color, one that appeals to the eye as well as the lips. Blues view the meal as an experience, a chance to say, "I'm glad you're here. Relax and get comfortable."

Greens are not typically adept at social situations. They will either talk about what's on their minds or something unique that you place before them. They will appreciate an opportunity to explore a unique entrée. They find interest in interesting people – people who think and who recognize cerebral connections.

Golds appreciate order and security. Don't surprise them with a lengthy period prior to your meal. Start courses on time. Don't surprise them with foods or eating utensils that they may not know how to use. If you remain in the dining room for dessert, they may think they should leave immediately following the meal. The move to the living room says, "Stay awhile and talk."

Oranges generally appreciate informality. If you overwhelm them with a for-mal dinner, you may not get a return invitation to their house. Your meal should be a bit daring but simple. Oranges will appreciate opportunities to do something as a part of their visit. Activities may stimulate conversation.

Remember to celebrate differences. Don't set out to change yourself or the person with whom you want to form a relationship. The real key to a positive relationship is for both parties to be who they are and to be able to do things that please the other member(s) of the relationship. The same balance that is necessary in your individual life can prove valuable in a relationship.

Often people find themselves attracted to other people who display a very different Color rainbow. For example, a Blue-Orange may find comfort in a Gold-Green's sense of purpose and direction. A Gold-Blue may find excitement in an Orange-Green's wry sense of humor and willingness to push the envelope. But will they appreciate one another's differences in six weeks or six years? Will they find as much interest in one another after the chase, or will they hope to change one another – to unleash their partner's Gold fetters or to tame the Orange beast?

It is important to know how well the two members of the relationship know themselves. It is also important to know how well they know one another. Do they see their differences as complements or as roadblocks? Do they want to change one another or come to know and appreciate one another at a deeper level? Are they willing to learn about one another's hot buttons, or will they be satisfied to use those buttons to manipulate one another?

Janice met Joe on a blind date, and it was love at first sight. Somehow Joe was different from anyone she had ever met. He drove a sports car, wore jeans instead of three-piece suits, and listened to loud rock and roll instead of classical music or jazz. When Janice was with Joe, she laughed. His antics could be a bit embarrassing at times, but they were also very freeing.

Janice's mother did not approve of Joe, however. He did not seem to want the same things that Janice wanted. He seemed to lack her focus, her drive, and her social graces. What worried her mother most was that Janice felt she could change Joe once they became more serious about one another. Janice felt that Joe loved her enough to change for her.

What You Bring to the Table

Will Joe change? Will Janice change? How much will each be willing to give? How much *should* each be willing to give?

These are just a few of the questions that you can ask yourself about the relationships you want to form. Now that you know your own Color order and can recognize the Colors in others, how can you use this knowledge to improve your personal relationships? How can you use this knowledge to set realistic expectations for yourself and other people with whom you want to develop a relationship? Before you consider the nuances of these and other questions, pause a moment to select a person with whom you want to form a better relationship. Use the Color identifiers on the next pages to clarify your similarities and differences. Don't forget that people with the same Color order will vary in their intensity due to their personal experiences.

What You Bring to the Table

From Color Identifiers To Color Comparisons

1. Place the Colors in the order of your own Color Rainbow
   (Blue, Gold, Green, Orange).

   _____

   _____

   _____

   _____

2. Place the Colors in the order of your friend's Color Rainbow
   (Blue, Gold, Green, Orange).

   _____

   _____

   _____

   _____

3. Is this your judgement of your friend's rainbow, or have your
   verified it with him/her?

   ☐ My judgement   ☐ I verified it

What You Bring to the Table

4. Place the two rainbows side by side in the table below.

My Rainbow	**Friend's Rainbow**

5. Does this comparison show you to be attracted to a person who is similar to or different from you?

   ☐ Someone similar to me   ☐ Someone different from me

6. What are the unique challenges presented by the similarities and differences in these rainbows?

   _____

   _____

   _____

7. After thinking about these similarities and differences, is this still a relationship that you want to develop further? Why or why not?

   _____

   _____

   _____

Recipes
& Menus

Recipes and Menus

So you want to get to know someone on a more personal level? Forming new relationships is like inviting someone to lunch. You think you might ask them, and yet you're not certain that they feel the same way you do. Will they politely say no? Will they feel obligated to say yes even if they don't want to join you? Should you risk inviting them to your home for lunch, or should you meet them at a restaurant – let the restaurant worry about the food and the ambiance so that you can put your efforts into getting to know one another? Will they like the same restaurants you frequent, or will they find them quaint or perhaps a bit ostentatious? Should the meal be formal or informal? What will you talk about? What should you wear?

Forming a relationship with another person requires some degree of risk. Relationships require common ground. I enjoy being with you because...

Judy understands personal relationships. She has what Howard Gardner (1993) calls interpersonal and intra-personal intelligence. She is highly skilled at understanding her own values and motivations as well as understanding the values and motivations of others. Judy loves everyone, and everyone loves Judy. In a room of fifty people Judy can make you feel as if you are the only person who matters. And by the end of the evening most of the fifty people in the room will have experienced that one-on-one connection with her.

Judy sees each day as a series of human relationships. The question of purpose, "Why is this important to this person?" drives her thoughts and actions. She is what Keirsey and Bates (1998) refer to as an idealist, an abstract cooperator, or intuitive-feeler. Judy is Blue.

Judy can make small talk as easily with the custodian at her daughter's elementary school as she can with a member of the town council. She sees people — not roles, occupations, or social status. Judy approaches every relationship in the same way, sensing what is important to the other person and automatically seizing that morsel to build meaningful connections. She throws formality and protocol aside so that she can see the world through the other person's eyes. And she is incredulous when others cannot establish such relationships.

Real relationships are Blue. You don't have to *be* Blue to have them, but at the very least you had better be able to *do* Blue effectively. Relationships are not equivalent to luck. They may begin as a chance encounter, but they don't develop by chance. They are built one step at a time. Let's look at them first as a Blue might see them. Then we will try to figure out how those of us whose Blue is a lesser part of our Color rainbow might learn to *do* the things necessary to develop relationship skills. It takes time and practice to develop a new set of skills. All of us are born with an inclination to certain skills or temperaments (Colors). Sometimes our family and friends value these Colors, and sometimes they do not. Too often we are criticized for those skills we don't demonstrate consistently rather than the ones we do. But you can learn to appreciate and improve your Color rainbow. And if you remain open enough to form relationships with other people, you can learn to complement one another's rainbows. Let's take a relationships chance and invite someone to lunch at our favorite restaurant.

The Real Relationships Menu

Almost 90% of the world sees relationships as something you get to when you finish other tasks. Remember, people whose primary color is Blue make up only 8-10% of the world's population.

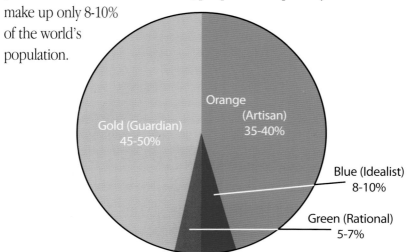

Golds *work* at relationships. Oranges may *avoid* relationships, especially if they are too confining. And Greens may *analyze* every aspect of a relationship until it loses its spontaneity.

Real relationships are built on a shared purpose. They require a commitment that runs to the heart of each partner in the relationship. My five-year-old granddaughter describes this as "the magic string that runs from my heart to your heart." Relationships are a matter of understanding rather than rules. But how do you come to know someone well enough to "know what is in their heart, let alone connecting that to your heart?

Stop a moment to consider the chart on page 27. What are the chances of your being born with Blue as your number one Color? They are roughly one in ten at best. Is it any wonder that meaningful human relationships are a scarce commodity? Again, every human being seeks positive personal relationships. But nine of every ten people do so only after they have satisfied other needs/demands. Those nine people may need to be reintroduced to their Blue.

Ed reminds his wife, Ellen, that he loves her very much, but he has a huge amount of responsibility as the CEO of a large company. He sends her flowers on her birthday and never forgets their anniversary. In fact, it hurts Ed that his wife questions his love. Can't she see that all of this – the house, the cars, the college tuition funds, and more – are for her and the kids?

Ellen says with sorrow in her voice that she does appreciate what Ed does for her and the kids. But she misses him. The kids miss him. More importantly, she adds, he is missing the kids. They are growing up before his very eyes, and he is missing it.

Recipes and Menus

I like to think of Real relationships as a menu that offers numerous choices around a central cuisine. They have a common purpose, or they would not exist. Yet, no menu would be complete without the appetizer, the salad, the side dishes, and the dessert. Figure 2.1 illustrates this relationships menu beginning with the appetizer and moving all the way through dessert. Notice how the menu builds like a menu at your favorite restaurant. It doesn't move directly to the main course. It begins with something light and tasty. You don't want the appetizer to fill you. You want it to peak your curiosity, to leave you wanting more.

The Real Relationships Menu
Figure 2.1

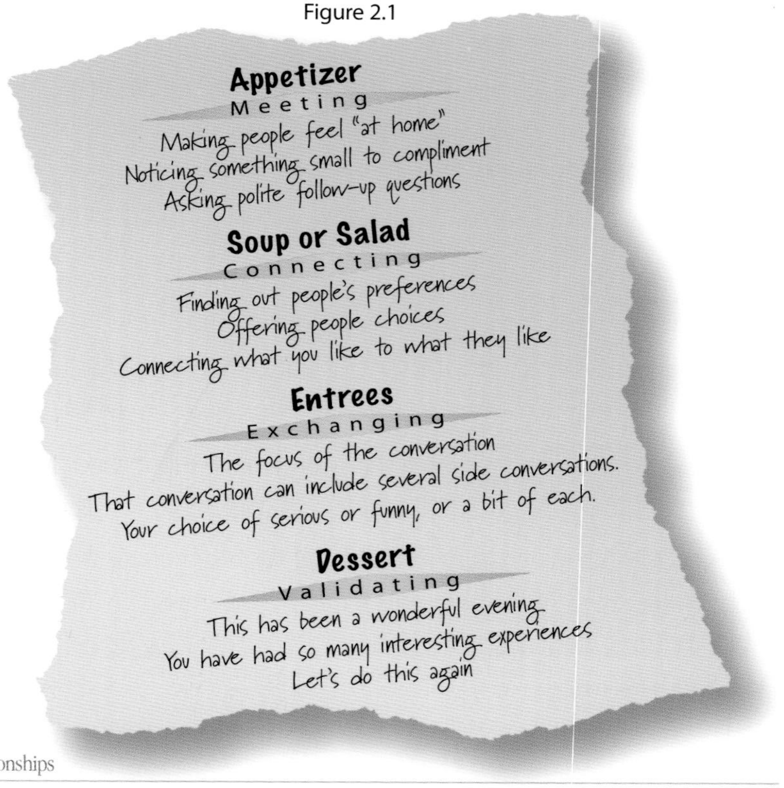

Appetizer
Meeting
Making people feel "at home"
Noticing something small to compliment
Asking polite follow-up questions

Soup or Salad
Connecting
Finding out people's preferences
Offering people choices
Connecting what you like to what they like

Entrees
Exchanging
The focus of the conversation
That conversation can include several side conversations.
Your choice of serious or funny, or a bit of each.

Dessert
Validating
This has been a wonderful evening
You have had so many interesting experiences
Let's do this again

The Real Appetizer

Few relationships begin with tough questions: are you a republican or a democrat or where do you go to church? And they also seldom begin with a lengthy description of yourself. We generally share the more personal details of our lives long after people make us feel at home — safe. We all want people to notice us, to notice what we like and to compliment our good taste: My, what a lovely coat. Blues know that these preliminary compliments can then be followed by easy questions: Is it as comfortable as it is beautiful? Did you find that at...? Do you shop there a great deal? All these questions are focused on the other person without making them feel uncomfortable.

Blues use relationship appetizers to welcome the other person to their world by telling them how much they appreciate their guests on a personal basis. They say, "I notice you and I want to know more about you." A Blue's initial comments and questions are typically light and noninvasive.

Real Soup or Salad

In relationships based on **Real Colors**®, you don't move directly from the appetizer to the main course. Blues know that once they have made their guest feel welcome, they will need to warm up to the conversation. You don't want to be rushed through a meal at your favorite restaurant. Blues let guests steer the conversation if they can: Tell me more about that. If there is more than one guest, Blues ask, "Do you enjoy ____ as much as Katy does, Jim? Isn't that fascinating how two people can be so different and yet enjoy some of the same experiences?" Such questions connect them to each guest and may connect various guests to one another. At the very least, Blues will make each person feel included in the conversation.

The Real Entrée

Once people feel at home (relaxed and comfortable) Blues know how to establish an initial focus to the conversation based on their guests' interests. If each guest has slightly different tastes, they move the conversation by alternating questions among topics (side dishes). They search for ways to tie one guest's experiences to another: *That is a fascinating experience. Did you find your trip to be anything like that, Tom?* (Each person has an opportunity to season the conversation according to their own tastes).

Blues understand that conversations are initiated and maintained more readily when people share common beliefs or experiences. Blues understand that planning the guest list is sometimes the first step in carrying off an effective dinner. They inquire about people's preferences prior to picking the restaurant. They know not to take Golds somewhere exotic for their first meal together, and they understand that Oranges hate to go to the same place twice. Likewise, they know that Greens will find it hard to be polite if they don't like either the food or the topic of conversation.

Real Dessert

Blues sense when people are getting full. They don't let conversations become invasive or overly serious. They recognize that Golds can stifle conversations with judgments and narrow viewpoints. They recognize that Greens can stifle conversations with lengthy descriptions and monotonous nuances and that Oranges can get carried away with stories of their own adventures with one story leading to another, and another, and...

Recipes and Menus

Blues recognize when someone has been quiet or uninvolved in the conversation. They know how to draw other people into the conversation without seeming to cut someone off. "That sounds just like the story you were telling me the other day, Betty. How did that go?" They also recognize how to draw the conversation to a close – how to leave guests wanting more.

But what happens after your initial dinner at a restaurant? Do you invite this person to your home? If so, how can you plan your menu? How can you make your guest feel welcome? Learning to *do* Blue is different from being born Blue. Some people seem to be natural cooks, while others require a recipe.

A Real Relationships Recipe

In the *Real Colors Homeowner's Guide* you learned how to take an inventory of your Real Colors stuff. Blue stuff (habits) can be collected in various ways. If I love people and am surrounded by family and friends who form lasting relationships with others, I am likely to gain a deep and meaningful understanding of relationships. If I am included in such relationships and encouraged to form friendships with people from varied backgrounds, my appreciation of human relationship skills will grow even stronger.

On the other hand, Gold stuff focuses on things like power, prestige, and wealth. If I find "things" more important to my long term survival than personal relationships and I am surrounded by family and friends who encourage and reward such behavior, I am likely to view success as collecting lots of "things." And I may limit my relationships to people who have things like my things or people who have things that I don't have.

Example: John was attracted to Sandy the first time they met. But he eventually found her to be a bit naive. She was beautiful, had a great smile, and seemed to be happy most of the time. But she seemed to think that fun just happened. She always wanted to go to expensive restaurants, to the theatre, or to a nightclub. She was seldom interested in talking about serious things. Sandy was a receptionist at a dentist office, and she seemed to be satisfied with her current salary – certainly an amount that would not satisfy John. John worried that Sandy's sense of satisfaction with her current lifestyle might indicate that she would not be willing to *work* at building the kind of life that he saw as important to their future relationship.

Green stuff includes ways of knowing how other stuff works, analyzing and dissecting things. If I have learned to enjoy taking things apart, I may find it more interesting to "take apart" my friends' ideas than to value and encourage relationships with them. I may tend to value people based on what they know rather than appreciating them for who they are.

Example: Greg enjoys his friend, Tim. But he wonders what Tim gets from their relationship. Tim doesn't seem to aspire to Greg's position. In fact, he talks about leaving the company soon. Perhaps he wants Greg to provide a reference for him. Or does he think Greg could be his connection – someone who will introduce him to another executive? Greg doesn't have many close friends, and he can't seem to shake this sense that Tim might be using him. Greg wishes he could *figure out* where Tim is coming from. He really enjoys being with Tim, but something doesn't add up with this relationship.

Recipes and Menus

Finally, Orange stuff includes competition and adventure, a love of games and entertainment. If I can afford to attend sporting events, to take risks and to see mistakes as learning opportunities, I may find all this relationship stuff as boring and monotonous. I may come to form friendships with people who share my thirst for adventure.

Example: Lisa is a sports nut. She is attracted to Dave, but she doesn't want to get tied down. She thinks she has a real chance to turn professional if she can stay focused on her golf game. Then she might consider getting more serious with Dave. Lisa wishes Dave would be more understanding of her situation. He can't seem to understand how much golf means to her. She needs time to practice, and she is often too tired after a long day on the golf course to go dancing. Lisa doesn't want to lose Dave, but he is just going to have to understand that she also loves golf.

If you don't have a large store of Blue stuff, you may find it difficult to entertain people who are not like you. But just because people like the same dish you do, don't assume they like it for the same reasons. Figure 2.2 illustrates that answers to the Four-P questions regarding a family dinner can be more of a smorgasbord than a menu.

A Menu of Responses in a Four-P Restaurant

Figure 2.2

Purpose:	Why is dinner an important meal?
Blue	It gives us time to share the joys and sorrows of our day.
Gold	Having dinner together establishes family traditions.
Green	It provides a consistent time for everyone to check-in on a daily basis.
Orange	It's the only time we pause from our busy schedules. That's when we talk.

Parameters:	What does a good meal look like?
Blue	The family sitting together talking about our day.
Gold	The family showing appreciation for what we have.
Green	The family sharing ideas and discussing significant world issues.
Orange	Who doesn't like a thick juicy steak and a healthy laugh around the family table?

Principles:	How can we vary the menu to suit everyone's tastes?
Blue	The menu doesn't matter nearly as much as the conversation.
Gold	Create a weekly set of menus so that everyone has a chance to choose a favorite meal.
Green	Give each person responsibility for planning one meal per week, and show them how they can contribute.
Orange	Give them what they like to eat and let them eat in front of the television once in awhile.

Priorities:	How can we make certain that everyone enjoys dinner?
Blue	Ask each person to share a happy experience from the day.
Gold	Teach them to be thankful for what they have and to be willing to share.
Green	Ask challenging open-ended questions that stimulate deep, rich conversations.
Orange	Serve something simple like pizza and focus your energy on having fun together.

Recipes and Menus

The fact that your primary Color is not Blue does not mean you can't answer a Blue question. You can learn a great deal by listening to people's answers to each of the Four-P questions. But you need to listen beyond the words themselves. Most of us provide a hint of our primary Color in our answers to all of the Four-P questions. Even if your primary Color is not Blue, you know why something is important to you.

Terry found herself in a series of short relationships that never seemed to develop into something deeper and more meaningful. She had many acquaintances but few real friends. Then she realized that she seldom got beyond lunch at her favorite restaurant. In only a few rare instances did these relationships develop to lunch at the other person's favorite restaurant. She began to wonder if she was expecting people to be like her before she could enjoy them. She had a difficult time enjoying people who did not enjoy the theatre, people who lacked an appreciation for community service, and people who saw life as a series of adventures.

If you find yourself in Terry's position, it may be time to move a relationship to the next level (from a meal at a restaurant to dinner at your place). Start out where you are comfortable – in your primary Color. However, as Figure 2.2 illustrates, people have different interpretations of the Four-P's. Learn to plan the meal around your own tastes, but be able to add a little less salt for a guest. Learn to hear the Blue compliment that is delivered with an Orange twist. After all, the recipe you have been using thus far has not seemed to work for you. Here are some easy steps to consider as you decide on the right relationship recipe to fit you and your guest.

1. Check your Real refrigerator and your Real food pantry. How much Blue stuff do you see?

2. If they are filled with primarily Gold, Green, or Orange stuff, you may need to find a simple Blue recipe. Perhaps you can ask a Blue friend for some help.

3. Remember, start with the stuff you already have on hand and then find the other ingredients you will need.

Now look at Figure 2.3 on the next page, and think about some of the ingredients you might want to consider as you build your relationship. After all, if you and your guest are going to enjoy this meal, it needs to include dishes that you both like.

a. Recognizing a Common Interest

The first ingredient for any Real relationship is recognizing something that you and the other person have in common. It may be a common hobby, a common place of employment, or a common activity. Now that you have shared a meal at the restaurant, you know more about one another. Do you share the same interests, or are you drawn together because of your differences?

Either similarities or differences can become the foundation for a meaningful relationship. But just like an individual Color, a combination of Colors in a relationship becomes a liability when it is carried too far. "I love you because you are so different from anyone I've ever known. Do that crazy thing you do...now wait a minute – I didn't mean to do it that much!"

In any lasting relationship there exists a bond, a common purpose that runs deeper than any one Color or behavior. Whether based on similarities or differences, a common purpose is more a matter of understanding than an adherence to rules. A shared purpose runs to the heart of

Figure 2.3

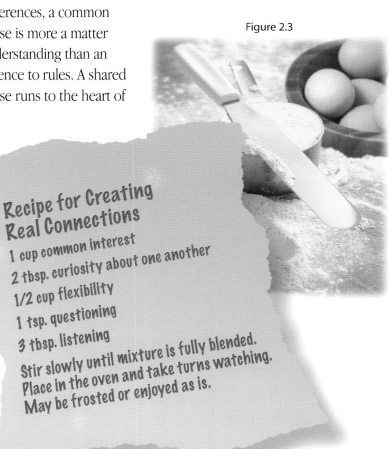

Recipe for Creating
Real Connections

1 cup common interest
2 tbsp. curiosity about one another
1/2 cup flexibility
1 tsp. questioning
3 tbsp. listening

Stir slowly until mixture is fully blended.
Place in the oven and take turns watching.
May be frosted or enjoyed as is.

any relationship. When a relationship forms at any level, the two parties must decide where to go next. Will they remain acquaintances or become friends?

b. Learning More About One Another

To grow a commitment or bond beyond a casual acquaintance, you need to learn more about the person. You need to show an interest in them by

Relationship Pathways
Figure 2.4

Getting To Know You...	
Responding	*Asking Questions*
Listening to their stories	**General**
Complimenting a Gold's hard work, a Blue's sense of creativity and wonder, a Green's ability to solve problems in unique ways, an Orange's wit and sense of adventure	And then what happened?
	Blue
	What is it about _____ that means so much to you?
	Gold
	How long did it take you to learn _____?
Sharing a similar experience without stealing the limelight	**Green**
	Do you think you could teach me to _____?
	Orange
	What's the next big adventure in your life?

tuning into their life events, their history, their joys and sorrows. You also need to risk sharing your life events with them. Figure 2.4 suggests some pathways to a deeper relationship.

Don't be offended if a Gold gives you a guarded answer to a question. Golds sometimes see questions as a way of making a judgment about them rather than as a way of getting to know them better. Don't be surprised if a Blue

Relationship Pathways
Figure 2.4

Well, I Really Enjoy...	
Responding	**Asking Questions**
Answering their questions about you	**General**
	Would you like to try _____ sometime?
Accepting their compliments with a thank you instead of an "Ah, shucks…"	**Blue**
	Can you see now how important that is to me personally?
Telling your stories without dominating the conversation	**Gold**
	Do you think you could teach me how to throw the day-timer away for a few days?
Sharing information without competing	**Green**
	Do you think you could teach a numbers person like me to enjoy a walk in the mountains without categorizing every plant?
	Orange
	Could you teach me to develop just an ounce of your patience?

gives you a much more esoteric answer than you think your question deserved. Blues see you and themselves as part of a "bigger story." Don't be surprised if a Green couches each segment of an answer so that you get a precise response to your question. Greens tend to be overwhelmingly logical and direct and often incapable of providing a "simple" answer. Don't be surprised if an Orange answers your question with a series of adventures. Oranges love to share their adventures and sometimes interpret a positive response as an invitation to share yet another adventure.

c. Sharing More Personal Information

Tom and Bob met one another at the car show. After a very positive conversation, they decided to share dinner at a nearby restaurant. During this dinner they learned that their shared interest ran deeper than restoring old cars. Both saw this hobby as a connection to their boyhood roots in the Midwest where they had worked on old cars with their fathers.

Mattie and Dave's common interest in cars, on the other hand, was somewhat different. Mattie was simply meeting her cousin who sold auto parts at the car show. By chance she happened to strike up a conversation with Dave, who was one of her cousin's best customers. Mattie fell in love with the stereo system in Dave's car, an afterthought for Dave, who simply wanted every possible gadget he could find for his "mean machine."

Tom and Bob shared a common interest in restoring cars. Whereas, Mattie and Dave seemed drawn to one another because of their differences. Mattie was intrigued that Dave took a quality stereo for granted. She loved music and was drawn to this "car nut" who lacked an appreciation for the beautiful music that played on his stereo. Likewise, Dave was drawn to this funny girl who noticed his stereo but lacked appreciation for the 1957 Corvette that housed it.

The recipe for Tom and Bob's relationship could turn out quite differently than Mattie and Dave's recipe. But neither relationship can go forward until the participants learn more about one another. What do you want to learn about your guest – how they are similar to you or how they are different? Perhaps you are hoping for a bit of both. Whatever draws you to this other person, you will eventually need to ask them some questions, to observe their behaviors, and to listen to the questions. You will need to watch their facial expressions and listen for the tone of their voice when they ask or answer a question. Do they sound excited or worried? Do their facial expressions seem relaxed or intent?

Eventually, you will want to know more about another person. But don't be content to make assumptions about body language or tone of voice. Test your assumptions. *"Your voice sounds tense. Are you worried or angry?"* or *"You look sad. Can I help in some way?"* If the relationship is to grow, you will both need to understand and appreciate one another's needs and interests. You can use the Four-P questions to build these connections. Of course, you should state them in your own words and chose the right time to ask them.

Purpose	Why do I find you to be an interesting person, and why do you find me interesting?
Parameters	What am I willing to share with you, and what are you willing to share with me at this point in the relationship?
Principles	How willing/able are we to let one another know when this relationship is not serving our individual and common needs?
Priorities	How committed are we to this relationship?

People usually structure questions and interpret answers from their own frame of reference. When Blues hear an answer to a "purpose" question, they may want to move on while both parties are in agreement. When Golds hear an answer to a "purpose" question, they may want to create parameters that ensure consistent expectations within the relationship. Greens may want to analyze what makes the relationship work, and Oranges may simply want to move directly to the next common adventure.

d. Sharing Responsibility For One Another's Needs

With any relationship recipe it is important to understand how each person is measuring and assessing the ingredients – how each person takes responsibility for growing the relationship. The Four-P measuring cup on the following page illustrates how people can learn to understand and appreciate the same meal from more than one perspective.

People measure satisfaction in numerous ways. Before you decide how much of any ingredient will go into your relationship recipe, you may want to consider the following.

- Know what both you and your guest expect from the relationship.

- Ask open-ended questions that clarify conflicting expectations.

- Listen *to* one another's answers rather than *for* the answers you expect.

- Make decisions based on what moves your relationship forward.

The Four-P Measuring Cup

That was a great meal because . . .

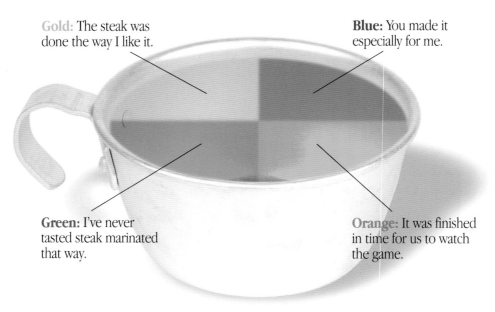

Gold: The steak was done the way I like it.

Blue: You made it especially for me.

Green: I've never tasted steak marinated that way.

Orange: It was finished in time for us to watch the game.

To a Blue parameters (Gold) *require* people to do something as opposed to developing a natural commitment to a shared interest or purpose. They believe that over analyzing a relationship (Green) gets in the way of "what really matters." They believe that competition (Orange) destroys camaraderie. But even most Blues would find value in asking the following questions.

Recipes and Menus

1. What are our expectations for this relationship?

2. What is each of us doing when the relationship is working?

3. How are we each contributing to the relationship?

4. Is this relationship worth further development?

These questions automatically imply change, but they shift the focus from a simple right or wrong to degrees of success – success in whose eyes, in which situations. They engage the collective energy of both individuals toward growing the relationship. They strengthen connections by clarifying issues that could otherwise divide people. They help the parties understand their individual and collective responsibilities for growing the relationship. They take the relationship beyond issues of compliance to issues of purpose by establishing a set of underlying principles that guide individual actions on a day-to-day basis. You won't develop the relationship skills you want to have by following one recipe. If you haven't taken the time to develop such skills in the past, you may need to develop a series of recipes that you can enjoy with different friends.

Before we consider a Real Relationships cookbook, however, take a moment to consider the questions on the following couple of pages to see if you have at least one or two recipes working for you.

The Real Recipe Checklist

1. With one person in mind, describe what a Real Relationship might look like in your world?

2. How would this other person describe a Real Relationship?

3. Is this your judgment of your friend's point-of-view, or have you verified it with him/her?

4. Do you see any conflict(s) between your two views? If so, what are they?

5. What are you willing to share with one another at this point in your relationship?

6. How willing are you and this person to tell one another when the relationship is not meeting your expectations?

7. Are you and this person committed to the relationship? Why, and how do you know this?

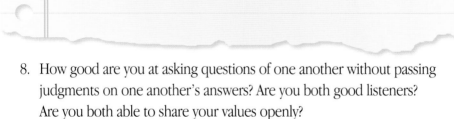

8. How good are you at asking questions of one another without passing judgments on one another's answers? Are you both good listeners? Are you both able to share your values openly?

Starting
with a
Cookbook

Starting with a Cookbook

My wife has a cookbook that her father gave her the first Christmas after we were married. Although it is now soiled, dog-eared, and missing some pages, it seldom sees the light of day. While Cynthia used it religiously during the first years of our marriage, her recipes now reside primarily in her head. My two sons and I like to say that *"Mom never makes a bad meal, but she never makes the same meal twice."* On a dreary day the soup may be a bit more spicy to *"bring some warmth into our world."* On a hot day the main entrée may be light so as not to weigh down our tired, oppressed bodies.

You often hear people say that they don't appreciate cookbook solutions to a problem. Give them individuality and uniqueness. But if you have little cooking experience, you may appreciate having a cookbook to get started. As time goes on, you can learn to add your own spices – season to taste.

This chapter is written for people who may not feel as comfortable as they would like to feel in the relationships kitchen – people who find Blue a little deeper in their Color order. It provides a cookbook for you to follow until you develop enough confidence to try your own recipes.

Real people are not all Blue. Neither are Real relationships. Real relationships are built on mutual expectations. Therefore, a real relationships cookbook must be more than a guide to your inner-Blue. Let's use Figure 3.1 to guide our cookbook discussion.

The Everything Cookbook (Wason, 1970) is divided into several parts: The ABC's of Food Preparation, Menu Planning and Weight Control, Recipes, etc.

Starting with a Cookbook

Figure 3.1

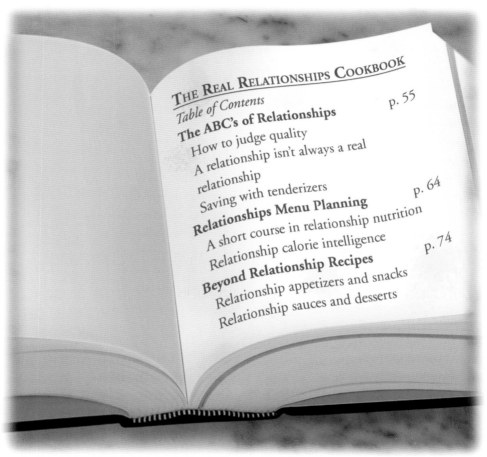

THE REAL RELATIONSHIPS COOKBOOK

The Real Relationships Cookbook can be similarly divided. First you need to understand what a relationship is. Then you need to understand how to build a basic relationship structure. Later you can add the sauces and desserts that keep your relationships exciting.

The ABC's of Relationships

Real relationships don't simply happen. They are built. How they are built determines their quality, their depth, and their duration.

a. How to Judge Quality

Quality falls inherently into our Gold temperament frame. Judgments require parameters – a closed set of guidelines that allow us to decide when something meets our standards. Your ability to judge the quality of a relationship depends on where these Gold characteristics fall within your temperament rainbow. If Gold is your primary or secondary color, you will likely be more able to define your expectations in your own mind and to share those expectations clearly with another person – sometimes too clearly. Let's take a look at how the position of your Gold attributes affects your ability to judge a relationship.

Jake is a CPA who knows what he is looking for in a relationship. He is a Gold-Green. Jake was raised in a very traditional home. He remembers very little about his father other than that he was at work a lot when Joe and his sister were growing up. Jake's father was an educator who worked two jobs when Jake was a toddler. He worked on a master's degree when Jake was in elementary school and was Jake's principal in high school.

Jake's mother was a teacher too. But she didn't work outside the home once Jake was born. In fact, she was a stay at home mom until Jake's younger sister went to junior high school. Jake remembers how his friends' had to go to daycare after school while he went home each day to a snack

Starting with a Cookbook

and an opportunity to share his daily adventures with "mom." His mother's sole reason to exist seemed to be to make Jake and his sister's life meaningful. Jake's house was alive with the sounds and smells of family life: laughter and teasing, beef stew, apple pie, holiday music and decorations. There was no such thing as a minor holiday within Jake's family. His mother had more Halloween decorations than most mothers had Christmas decorations. She sang in the church choir, hauled the kids to dance lessons and football practice, and nightly tucked "her babies" into bed.

Even when Jake was in college, he remembers his mother waiting up for him on a weekend over vacations. She would pretend to be sleeping when Jake arrived home well after midnight. He would make just enough noise to let her pretend that he had awakened her. Then she would fix him a snack and listen to his problems and adventures – never prying, but always interested.

That's what Jake is looking for in a relationship. He knows most women will want to have a career, and he is resigned to his wife working part time after the children are born. But he wants to find a person who will place family above career so that his children can know the love and stability he knew as a child.

Hauney, on the other hand, is a successful attorney whose Gold falls third on her rainbow order. Hauney is a Green-Orange adopted by a middle-aged couple who had been unable to conceive children. Hauney was

the center of her parents' lives, an only child who was bright and outgoing. Hauney's mother was a psychologist. Her father was an attorney. Both were able to rearrange their schedules to attend Hauney's dance recitals, her gymnastics competitions, and every
parent conference including parents' weekends in college.

Hauney cannot imagine sitting at home while her husband "takes care" of her and the family. She will help at school and attend school events. But she cannot picture herself as a room mother or a PTA president.

What happens when Jake and Hauney meet? Will they be attracted to one another? Can they have a relationship? Will it last?

There are no easy answers to these questions. But let's consider for a moment what we mean by a relationship.

b. A Relationship Isn't Always a Relationship

We spend most of our waking hours contemplating relationships. After all, no one wants to go through this life alone. Willie Nelson (1994) tells us, however, that there are worse things than being alone. Two people do not necessarily constitute a relationship – at least not a Real Colors relationship. Often relationships are little more than what Jean Piaget (1952) long ago described as "parallel play." Figure 3.2 illustrates the difference between a Real Colors Relationship and parallel play.

Parallel play involves two or more children engaged in a series of events that happen simultaneously and in close proximity to one another with little or no direct interaction. For example, two toddlers or kindergarten children

Figure 3.2

may be very excited to have a play date. To untrained adults they may appear to be playing something together. But under closer examination, it becomes apparent that they are engaged in two different activities with little or no connection to one another. Both children might be playing with cars but not interacting with one another in any way.

Adult "relationships" can be very similar to these parallel play experiences. One adult is intrigued by the other and begins to ask questions. Often it is differences rather than similarities that attract them. Let's take Jake and Hauney, for example.

Suppose Jake and Hauney meet at a party. They are initially attracted to one another through a conversation regarding local politics. Both support a candidate for mayor who is a visionary, a person who wants to bring new opportunities to their town – not just new businesses, but cultural and educational opportunities. As Jake and Hauney talk, they are both fascinated and perplexed by the other. Jake admires Hauney's intelligence and wit. She is warm and fun and shows interest in him in much the same way that his mother always did. Yet, something about Hauney seems different. Jake is impressed by her leadership skills and at the same time somewhat over-whelmed by her forcefulness. Hauney strikes Jake as a bit too opinionated, a bit too aggressive – charming but not as warm as he had grown to expect women to be.

Hauney is struck by Jake's depth of knowledge about city finances and how they could be leveraged to accomplish the things that the mayoral candidate wants to accomplish. She is impressed by Jake's self-confidence and his steady approach to problem solving. At the same time, Hauney finds Jake a bit controlling. He seems to be more interested in impressing her than truly listening to her ideas and opinions. Once he gets his mind made up, it is difficult for anyone to change it. It is as though Jake thinks he has the right solution for any problem and expects other people to be as excited about that solution as he is. Jake seems to have a tool kit full of solutions just wait-ing for a problem to solve. To Hauney, Jake is somewhat like her Uncle Ray, a person her father used to call, "Ray One Way." Her father said that to Uncle Ray there was only one way to do things – Ray's way.

Jake and Hauney's "relationship" represents how temperament and experience combine to influence our personality, our way of looking at life. Notice how their Colors both unite and challenge them. They are attracted to one

another's Green – the abstract side of the house. But they are somewhat befuddled by their differences in terms of the concrete side – Jake's Gold and Hauney's Orange. What is it in their backgrounds that affects the way they act from their own Colors and influences how they respond to one another? If they continue their relationship for any period of time (regardless of whether it is professional or personal) it could become little more than parallel play. What are their choices at this point?

c. *Saving With Tenderizers*

Sometimes a filet mignon that looked great in the butcher's display case can turn out to be a bit tough when you get it home. Yet, all is not lost at that point. You can still enjoy its exquisite taste if you can get beyond its tough exterior. There are various ways to tenderize a relationship if you think it might be worth the effort.

Real Color differences can provide an attraction and can even be a reason for celebration. But you must first understand them in order to appreciate them. Few relationships are truly "made in heaven." They require a relationship tenderizer. Conversation provides the tenderizer in a relationship – conversation that requires non-judgmental questions and honest responses. Real relationship conversations are more than chitchat. They provide opportunities to ask questions about the other person's preferences – their joys, fears, dreams, memories, and disappointments. They require a willingness to risk and a commitment to honor your partner's confidences.

Let's return to Jake and Hauney for a moment. We know their Color preferences. Jake is a Gold-Green, and Hauney is a Green-Orange. But a person's color preferences tell only part of their story. If you are going to build a mutually positive relationship with another person, you need to know how their experiences have shaped their lives. Don't assume that their experiences were similar to yours even if you think you have come from "similar backgrounds."

Both Jake and Hauney grew up in homes where they were the center of their parents' lives. But unlike Jake, Hauney had the full attention of both parents. She had many chances to observe and participate in her parents' relationship. Remember that Hauney's father and mother could arrange their schedules to be an active and "present" force in Hauney's life. Jake's father, on the other hand, had been an active yet indirect participant in Jake's life. When Jake was young, his father held a teaching position during the day and went to graduate school at night. When his father was home, he was often studying for class. When Jake was a teenager, his father was gone several nights a week at school activities. Even though he could attend Jake's high school sports activities, Jake had to share his father's attention with other students. To be one of the guys, Jake often had to meet friends' expectations at the risk of disappointing or even embarrassing his father. In such situations it was often Jake's mother who seemed to love and defend him regardless of whether he was right or wrong.

Jake and Hauney both came from loving, stable homes. But their parents had modeled two very different relationships for and with them. Neither one was more right than the other – just different. Hauney's parents both worked. Jake's mother stayed at home. Hauney's father helped with house-hold chores, but Jake's father was often at school on nights and weekends when household chores were being completed. Hauney's mother and father cooked meals together. Often they would share a cup of coffee and dance between the refrigerator and the range as they cooked – laughing and including Hauney in this family ritual. Jake's parents often sipped a cup of tea and danced in the kitchen too. But since Jake's father often arrived home past Jake's bedtime, Jake didn't often participate in these activities.

Jake and Hauney are a typical example of two people who seem to have a great deal in common. Neither was abused nor neglected. But each one learned a slightly different recipe for achieving a happy, stable, and loving home life. It is not enough to ask another person what they value. You need to ask them *what that value looks like in action*. You have to tenderize the filet in order to enjoy its hidden flavor. The Four-P questions provide a useful tenderizer to help two people build a flavorful relationship.

Purpose:	Why is this important to you and to me?
Parameters:	What does it look like to each of us based on our life experiences (how have we learned to look at it)?
Principles:	How can we adjust our individual expectations to meet our common goals?
Priorities:	Where do we start to ensure the greatest likelihood of building a relationship that is meaningful and fulfilling to both of us?

When individuals share a confidential piece of their life, their partners/friends need to suspend judgment and ensure confidentiality of the information with which they have been entrusted. This builds what

Starting with a Cookbook

Covey (1989) calls an emotional bank account. "You are someone I can trust to care about me, to listen to me, and to honor my beliefs as well as my privacy." Let's explore how you can build such emotional bank accounts with another person.

Relationships Menu Planning

Real relationships are chosen and cultivated, regardless of how they begin. To cultivate a relationship, you need to understand relationship nutrition. What makes a relationship healthy and vital?

a. Relationship Nutrition

When two people enter into a relationship, each brings something to the table. Since we have said that relationships are a Blue undertaking, you might think that a Blue has a greater chance than a Green, an Orange, or a Gold of achieving a healthy relationship. But alas this is not the case. Csikszentmihalyi (1990) tells us that we seldom achieve happiness by seeking it. Unfortunately for many Blues who are highly sensitive to matters of purpose and relationships, nothing seems to measure up to their expectations.

John is a Blue who is highly sensitive and extremely aware of people's feelings. John meets few people in this world that he cannot befriend. He overlooks people's frailties and sees beyond their vices, choosing to see who they could be rather than who they are. With such affection and devotion for those around him, you might think that John would have many close friends. But the opposite is true.

Starting with a Cookbook

No one can live up to John's expectations. People depend on him to be there in any situation, but they are frequently absent when John needs them. They often see John as naive and unfocused – great to be around at a social event but short on drive and personal motivation. John prefers being to doing, casual conversation to problem solving protocols. He is a talented writer, but he has little time for grammatical formalities. John gives himself completely to any relationship and loses his own identity in his efforts to be what other people need him to be. John, like many Blues, often becomes so concerned about nourishing other people through a relationship that he neglects his own nutritional needs.

To understand this dilemma, imagine for a moment the warning on an airline safety video regarding the emergency deployment of the oxygen masks.

The sign reminds passengers to employ their own masks before trying to help someone else. John and many other Blues might find themselves oxygen starved because they neglect their own needs in order to serve others. A Real relationship thrives only when both parties bring something of value to the table and take something of value with them when they leave the table. Real relationships depend on a dynamic balance. They are not 50-50. Sometimes they are 95-5 and later 5-95. In Real relationships one partner does not insist on a fair share simply because it is available. Real partners recognize when they need more nutrition, and they ask for it. Likewise, they recognize when the other partner needs it, and they make it available.

b. Relationship Calorie Intelligence

Howard Gardner (1993) suggests that human beings are not cursed with a single form of intelligence called Intelligence Quotient (I.Q.). Rather, we are blessed with multiple intelligences. Two of these types of intelligence that are extremely important to effective relationships are intra-personal intelligence and interpersonal intelligence. Intra-personal intelligence involves an individual's ability to know and understand his/her own abilities and needs – strengths and liabilities. Interpersonal intelligence involves people's ability to recognize strengths and liabilities in other people and to know how to interact with others in a way that is mutually beneficial to both parties. In a Real relationship both parties need to monitor how much energy they take from the relationship (the relationship calories they take from the other person) as well as the energy they bring to the relationship (the calories they contribute to the other person).

Starting with a Cookbook

The calorie chart illustrated in Figure 3.3 provides a starting point for thinking about relationships. For illustrative purposes it deals with individual colors rather than the entire color rainbow. If the explanations following the chart seem simplistic, they are. In real life human beings are not a single color. We possess a complete rainbow of colors. For example, a Green-Gold might react differently in a personal relationship than a Green-Orange. A Blue-Gold might react differently than a Blue-Orange, etc. However, since we lead with our primary color, let's try to isolate those personality characteristics now. We will discuss the nuances of color rainbows in later chapters.

Personal Relationships Calorie Chart
Figure 3.3

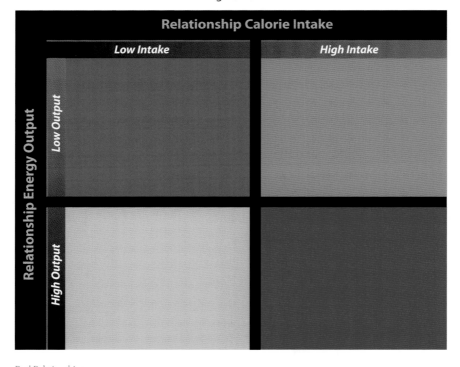

Starting with a Cookbook

The labels in the top row or horizontal axis of this chart indicate the amount of relationship calories that you require from a relationship – what you take away for your survival. The labels in the left column or vertical axis indicate the energy or attention that you bring to the relationship.

Greens neither seek a tremendous amount of personal relationship calories (input) nor produce a tremendous amount of relationship energy (output). Blues, on the other hand, need high quantities of relationship calories and generate equally high quantities of relationship energy.

Greens are thinkers who often connect more with ideas and concepts than with people. Their idea of a good time involves problem solving. Greens often like to work alone so that they can control the variables in any problem situation. They feel uncomfortable sharing too much personal information that might be misinterpreted by people with a less discerning eye – information that might be used against them later. They tend to qualify or even limit their output of personal/emotional words and actions. Greens often seem distant or aloof. They want to be appreciated for their ability to see unique connections among highly complex ideas, tasks, and concepts. They like to make their contributions to a relationship by providing insights and strategic solutions. They have trouble letting go of logic and truth in order to deal with the emotional side of a relationship.

Blues see their world in terms of human relationships and a sense of a higher purpose in life. Blues expect other people to be sensitive to their feelings and willing to judge their intentions rather than their actions. They feel uncomfortable when people hold back information or feelings. They care deeply about a person's intentions and can overlook flaws in a product that comes from the heart. But they expect people to act on their intentions in an open and expressive manner. Where a Green might be described as aloof, a Blue might be described as effusive – too much information. They seem at times to repeat themselves to be certain that people *feel the purpose* underlying their words and actions.

Alan is a Green. Monique is a Blue. After fifteen years of marriage, Monique has learned to tell Alan when she needs sympathy and compassion. In the early years of their relationship, Monique would share her problems from work in the expectation that Alan would be sympathetic and defend her as

right, if not righteous. However, the ever-logical Alan would often point out how Monique might have avoided this problem altogether by using more logic herself. At times he almost seemed to take her boss's side in these matters. What Monique wanted was unquestioning sympathy and understanding. What she received from Alan was a litany of questions designed to elicit a logical solution to her problem.

This was a situation in which a low emotional input/low emotional output Green could not provide the emotional support that Monique needed. On the other hand, Alan actually voiced a sense that Monique was sending him mixed signals. After all, Monique always praised his ability to be objective under pressure. Why was it inappropriate for him to use his logic in solving *her* problems? Did Monique expect Alan to be untruthful?

No, Monique expected Alan to be empathetic rather than logical. She expected him to understand that these moments were about her feelings — not simply another logical problem for Alan to solve.

Eventually Monique learned to tell Alan when she needed him to listen, when she wanted sympathy more than a solution. When she did this, Alan was able to suspend his problem solving and replace logic with a sympathetic ear and a reassuring hug. He learned eventually to ask Monique how she felt and why the situation bothered her so much. And he also learned to say simply, *"I'm sorry you had a bad day. I love you. Why don't you put some soft music on the stereo while I fix dinner."*

Greens neither seek a tremendous amount of personal relationship calories (emotional input) nor produce a tremendous amount of relationship energy (emotional output).

However, they expect their relationship partners to recognize those rare moments when they need empathy and reassurance. Blues, on the other hand, need high quantities of relationship calories and generate equally high quantities of relationship energy. And there is no question that they view empathy and concern as the starting point for any relationship.

Now let's turn our attention from the Abstract Blues and Greens to the Concrete Golds and Oranges. Golds want to belong to a group and will do so even if they don't like the group(s) available to them. To belong to a group you don't like is better than being alone. Oranges, on the other hand, don't generally want to be limited by a group. They want to enjoy many experiences that require group interaction, but they may find that group rules, deadlines, and expectations limit their freedom – their opportunities for adventures where they can demonstrate their unique talents.

Golds are scouts, committee members, etc. They work at a relationship, and they expect their relationship partners to do the same. Golds prefer to be recognized for their contributions through concrete rewards: good grades, higher pay, special awards, etc. They may become embarrassed by effusive praise or even find it disingenuous. Telling a Gold that they did a good job is fine, but they want you to demonstrate your appreciation in concrete ways.

Starting with a Cookbook

Golds often value hard work that results in a mediocre product more than a perfect product that someone discovered by chance.

Oranges see the world as a series of adventures. If you recognize Oranges today, they want to prove that they can deliver an even better product tomorrow. People often interpret Orange behavior as bragging or showing-off. But to an Orange life is having fun. It is a game – I win today and you win tomorrow. The objective is not winning or losing. It is playing the game to the best of your ability. Orange jokes and antics, rather than being self-serving, are designed to make people feel good. Oranges enjoy life and can appreciate a joke whether they play it on someone else or someone else plays it on them.

Luis, a Gold traffic cop, was married to Francesca, an Orange restaurateur. Both partners to this relationship had a high need to achieve. But Luis was an extremely loyal family man. After a busy day at work, he wanted to spend time at home with the kids. Francesca, on the other hand, needed to unwind. Often she would be late for dinner, and it was not at all unusual for her to plan a golf outing with a patron instead of attending her kids' plays or soccer games.

The first years of their marriage had been exciting and entertaining. Luis had enjoyed Francesca's sense of adventure. She had appreciated his solid sense of right and wrong and his willingness to organize or even rescue her week-end adventures. But after the kids came along, Luis and Francesca seemed to drift apart. He seemed less and less approving of her risky raft trips and careless hikes with the kids. She seemed to grow tired of his judgments and his monotonous routines.

Starting with a Cookbook

In the midst of a stormy argument one evening, Luis simply said, "Francesca, I love you. The kids and I need you. And too often you simply aren't there for us. Your restaurant will be there forever, but the kids won't."

Both Monique and Alan's relationship and Luis and Francesca's relationship required some revitalization – some balance. It is often easy for partners to take one another for granted, to take more from a relationship than they give. Sometimes you count so much on a partner to fill a place in your Color rainbow that you forget how to exercise that aspect within your own temperament repertoire. You find yourself on one side or the other of the calorie balance – either giving more to the relationship than you are receiving or taking more than you are giving. You are either overfeeding or underfeeding the relationship. In either case you are not nourishing it. What you need is to go beyond the relationship recipes that you have come to depend on. Even tasty recipes can become monotonous.

Beyond Relationship Recipes

From time to time any relationship may be dragged down by the strain of everyday life: too much excitement or too little, too much togetherness or not enough. At times like this, it may help to remember what made the relationship work in the first place. What is it that you used to do when you first met? What were those little things you did before you got ready for a date? Do you still wear makeup when you go out? Does he wear a nice sweater to dinner or that old flannel shirt?

When people first meet, they want to impress one another. Perhaps they have a special perfume they wear. Perhaps there is a restaurant or a little gift that makes the evening special. These are the appetizers that get another person interested in us, the snacks that tide us over from one major event to the next.

a. Appetizers and Snacks

Appetizers and snacks are not designed to nourish us. They are designed to alert our appetite to something yet to come or to calm our appetite between meals. Appetizers and snacks exist outside the main course. In a Real relationship these appetizers and snacks are comprised of the common little kindnesses that partners do for one another – gestures of recognition or invitation.

Starting with a Cookbook

An old saying reads, "Familiarity breeds contempt." Think about your own relationships. Have you noticed that when you get to know another person, you sometimes overlook the relationship appetizers and snacks that were so common in the early days of your relationship? Why do you no longer excuse yourself from the table, send your partner a small gift for absolutely no reason, ask about his or her day, compliment an outfit, or insist that they choose the restaurant or movie for the evening's entertainment?

These are the appetizers and snacks of a relationship. Golds often excuse themselves from preparing their own appetizers and snacks. They can become so focused on the main entrée and meal logistics (their responsibilities) that they overlook the nuances related to atmosphere (relationships). Greens are practical. They mean to do the extras, but they get preoccupied with the reasons underlying the meal (long-term strategies that will eventually pay for the kids' college tuition or lead to that promotion at work). They sometimes appear to overlook the personal needs of the people at the table. Oranges can get so excited about their guests having a good time that they also overlook the details. They can spend so much energy on the special occasions (that round of golf with a friend) that they overlook the "in between moments."

Blues see each aspect of the meal as important: colors, aromas, and unique presentations that say, *"I wanted to do something special for you."* To Blues anytime is a "Hallmark moment" if you take the time to appreciate it. But you don't need to be Blue to do Blue.

Whether in a friendship or a family situation, most of us still appreciate those little relationship appetizers, those things that our friends and spouses don't have to do but do anyhow. Larry never forgets a friend or colleague's birthday. Fong never fails to compliment a friend's outfit or haircut. Joey opens doors for male or female friends and helps anyone with a coat. Real relationship appetizers and snacks are somewhat generic. They really know no particular Color. A Green can show as much appreciation as a Gold through the same relationship appetizer or snack. An Orange can astound a Blue with an appetizer or snack that usually comes from an unexpected direction.

But appetizers and snacks do not replace an entrée. In fact, they are somewhat separate from it. Kindnesses of any kind mean something to most of us regardless of our age, gender, or temperament. But what are those special sauces and desserts that tell a person you know and appreciate them on a more personal level? These are the extras that make a partner in any relationship feel as if they are the only person in the room, the focus of the party.

b. Sauces and Desserts

Real relationships are incomplete without sauces and desserts. Like a sauce, each individual in the relationship flavors or completes the other person's life in some manner or form. Each person gives something to the other. And like a dessert, the relationship offers a dynamic balance that goes beyond nutritional requirements. You could skip dessert without neglecting your nutritional needs. A Real relationship dessert is the extra — that part of the meal that no one needs nutritionally but most of us enjoy emotionally. A special sauce can hide the taste of a prime rib that was overcooked. A special dessert can erase its memory altogether.

Let's think about relationship sauces for a moment. We all have a unique sauce that we bring to the table. What is your special relationship sauce? Figure 3.4 illustrates the recipe for the sauce that each color brings to a relationship.

The important thing to remember about a relationship sauce is to *offer* it, make it available. Sometimes your partner does not want the sauce you provide. In fact, too much sauce destroys the taste of a prime cut of meat. People may pay so much attention to the sauce that they lose sight of the entrée itself. When you add your sauce to a relationship, ask yourself, *"Whose need does this sauce satisfy: your need or your partner's?"* As you grow in your relationship, you will learn how much sauce they want or need, when they want it, and whether they want it added directly to the situation at hand or prefer it on the side.

Color Sauces
Figure 3.4

Blues offer...	*Tenderness and emotions to*	Stable Golds, problem solving Greens, and energetic Oranges
Golds offer...	*Stability and consistency to*	Emotive Blues, problem solving Greens, and energetic Oranges
Greens offer...	*Analysis and problem solving to*	Emotive Blues, stable Golds, and energetic Oranges
Oranges offer...	*Energy and adventure to*	Emotive Blues, stable Golds, and problem solving Greens

The same is true of a Real relationship dessert. As two people progress through situations at work, at home, or in social settings, they learn how to combine their talents in ways that go beyond what either might accomplish separately. Real relationships add something to both people's lives. You learn to appreciate one another, to recognize one another's strengths, to support one another's dreams and aspirations. You learn how to add to one another's life with a special dessert rather than trying to overcome one another's shortcomings with emotional sauces. Partners in a Real relationship create more calories than either one needs individually, more calories than they need together. At their best, Real relationships create beautiful desserts that can be shared with and enjoyed by other people. They draw people to them.

To know whether your relationship is ready for dessert, you might ask the following questions.

- Is this relationship built on a mutual sense of purpose that evolves from each individual's sense of purpose?

- Does this relationship involve enough stability for us to practice and expand our skills and talents?

- Do we think about our day-to-day decisions in ways that align our individual actions with our mutual sense of purpose?

- Do our actions bring energy and enthusiasm to the relationship so that we continue to grow together?

Remember, it is okay (in fact, desirable) to *be* your own Color. But you need to be able to *do* all of the Colors. You may not be able to organize a dinner party alone, but could you pick up the groceries, set the table, or clear the dishes from the table? You may not have numerous travel adventures to share, but could you ask questions about another person's travels, comment positively about their point-of-view, or compliment their sense of humor? You may not know how to initiate a scintillating conversation with another person, but could you avoid showing your disapproval of their comments, redirect the conversation to another person, or laugh and move onto another topic?

Starting with a Cookbook

Partners in a Real relationship plan their recipes and menus together. They know what they bring to the table, and they use their talents to add to the relationship meal. They also recognize what they don't bring to the table, and they aren't afraid to depend on other people for those dishes. Before we move to entertaining other people within a relationship, take a moment to review your use of the Relationship Cookbook.

Using a Relationships Cookbook

1. Using the *Personal Relationships Calorie Chart* below, place a letter *S* for self and a letter *P* for a relationship partner in the square that describes each person's calorie input and energy output. (Refer to pages 67-68 of this chapter for background.)

Personal Relationships Calorie Chart

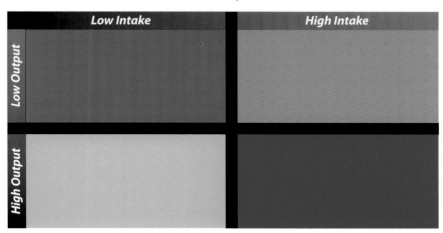

	Low Intake	High Intake
Low Output		
High Output		

2. What are the "nutritional" implications of your answer in item one to your relationship with this person?

3. What are some of the appetizers and snacks that typify your relationship with this person?

Appetizers and Snacks I Provide	Appetizers and Snacks My Partner Provides

4. What are some of the sauces and desserts that typify your relationship with this person?

Sauces I Provide	*Sauces My Partner Provides*
Desserts I Provide	*Desserts My Partner Provides*

5. Using the chart below, place a letter *S* for self and a letter *P* for a relationship partner in the square that describes the sauces that each person brings to the relationship table. (Refer to pages 77-78 of this chapter for background.)

Color Sauces

Blues offer...	*Tenderness and emotions to*	Stable Golds, problem solving Greens, and energetic Oranges
Golds offer...	*Stability and consistency to*	Emotive Blues, problem solving Greens, and energetic Oranges
Greens offer...	*Analysis and problem solving to*	Emotive Blues, stable Golds, and energetic Oranges
Oranges offer...	*Energy and adventure to*	Emotive Blues, stable Golds, and problem solving Greens

6. What are the implications of your answer in item five to your relationship with this person? (Think in terms of what you both bring to the table as well as what sauces may still be missing.)

Starting with a Cookbook

Your
Relationship
Glass

Your Relationship Glass
Focusing on How Full Rather than How Empty

Almost a half century ago Victor Frankl (1959) suggested that the most important thing we choose in our life is our attitude. All too often we fail to question the assumptions underlying those attitudes or to understand the experiences that may have strengthened or weakened them over time.

Take a moment to think about some of the most fundamental beliefs and attitudes that shape your life today. Can you recall any life experiences or combination of life experiences that may have shaped these beliefs and attitudes? Can you honestly say which beliefs and attitudes you have simply taken for granted (for example, something you may have learned from parents or friends) and which you have adopted based on careful thought and analysis?

The purpose of this chapter is to help you think about your personal relationships in terms of all the positives you and your partner bring to them. That is, you need to develop the habit of seeing how full your Relationship glass is rather than how empty. Take a look at Figure 4.1. It represents two people: one who is Gold-Blue and the other who is Green-Gold.

Did you focus on the fact that this glass contained three of the four Colors: Blue, Green, and Gold? Or did you

The Relationship Glass
Figure 4.1

Your Relationship Glass

Focusing on How Full Rather than How Empty

focus on the fact that it was missing Orange? Did you see the cup as three-quarters full or one-quarter empty? Let's consider what happens when people see their Relationship glass as partially empty rather than almost full.

Seeing What's in the Glass Rather than What Isn't

Nearly 2500 years ago Cicero was beheaded for pointing out to the Roman people what he referred to as the six mistakes of man. Take a moment to review the modern wording of Cicero's list below. How often do you find yourself making one or more of these mistakes?

Mistake #1   Thinking of life in terms of winners and losers

Mistake #2   Worrying about things over which you have little control

Mistake #3   Assuming that no answer exists because you don't know what it is

Mistake #4   Settling for what you know without considering what might be possible

Mistake #5   Failing to read and learn about new ideas

Mistake #6   Attempting to force others to believe and live as you do

How do these mistakes evolve through each of our Colors. The following paragraphs provide general examples of Color attributes in terms of these mistakes. As you read them, keep in mind that they are examples, not absolute descriptors.

a. What Mistake #1 Looks Like

Mistake #1, thinking of life in terms of winners and losers, appears most obviously among concretes: Golds and Oranges. These individuals see the world as finite. There is only so much to go around. Golds want to protect what they have and to choose with whom they share it. Oranges want to get their share before someone else comes along and hoards it. However, Oranges are more likely than Golds to share their prizes since they soon tire of them and want to make room for new prizes.

Abstracts (Blues and Greens) are more subtle when they engage in Mistake #1. Greens need to have people recognize that they think and problem solve better than anyone else. They win by making other people look silly or naive. Blues generally wait a long time before resorting to thoughts of "winning and losing." But when they have been pushed too far and ignored or embarrassed for wearing "rose-colored" glasses, Blues can rip out another person's heart. Greens use humiliation and sarcasm to win. Blues use righteous indignation.

b. What Mistake #2 Looks Like

Like the first mistake, **Mistake #2, worrying about things over which you have little control,** is not unique to any one Color. We all have a tendency to worry about those things that we cannot change or "fix." Blues worry about any tense situation. They worry when one individual is unhappy. Greens worry that people are too emotional, too inclined to follow a charismatic person without asking questions, or too quick to jump to solutions without taking the time to identify the problem. Blues want everyone to connect with other people on a personal level. Greens want people to learn how to solve their own problems.

Golds and Oranges worry about concrete things. Golds worry that people aren't willing to work hard enough or that they are not willing to sacrifice for the greater good. Oranges worry about fences: rules that get in their way. They worry that if people become too dependent on others, they will lose that "pioneering, can-do spirit."

c. What Mistake #3 Looks Like

Mistake #3, assuming that no answer exists because you don't know what it is, occurs most often when people believe their Color attributes are unappreciated or under-appreciated. This sense of despair sounds some- what similar among all the Colors. *"People just don't understand...it's fruitless to...people just don't get it...no one seems to care that..."* The differences come in what follows these openers. Blues lament the fact that people ignore the good in others or that they want to take more than they give. Golds echo the "taking more than they give," but they add, "I can't do it all." Greens lament that it's useless to talk about logic in a "sound-bite" world. Oranges express outrage that they are tired of being hassled, fed-up with senseless regulations, etc.

The interesting thing about Mistake #3 is that it causes people to believe they have more in common than they actually do. They unite to "throw out the scoundrels" only to find themselves fighting internally when they realize how little they actually have in common. Once they "throw out the scoundrels" they no longer share a common interest.

d. What Mistake #4 Looks Like

Mistake #4, settling for what you know without considering what might be possible, is often an outgrowth of Mistake #3. It is expressed in the adage, "The devil is in the details." Most of us can agree on a common set of life values. For example, most people express a belief in truth, hard work, and caring for the oppressed. But we may act on these values in vastly different ways.

When we make Mistake #4 we get caught up in our worst fears. "No one sees this situation the way I see it. If I don't insist on more Blue, Gold, Green, or Orange (fill in the blank with your primary Color) 'they' will simply give lip-service to 'my' concerns." Blues can't get enough reassurance that a problem solution will address personal relationships. Golds can't get enough reassurance that people will assume individual responsibility for implementing the solution. Greens will never be satisfied that the solution can address every contingency and that the implementation strategy includes opportunities to monitor and adjust procedures. Oranges want action now. They "know" that people are afraid to act, to act in immediate and unique ways.

e. What Mistake #5 Looks Like

At first glance **Mistake #5, failing to read and learn about new ideas,** sounds Green and Gold. But once again this mistake knows no Color boundaries. The nuances lie in what each Color believes to be worth reading and learning about. Blues might recommend reading self-help and personal growth books. They might ask us to spend more time learning how to relate to one another and considering how our actions affect our personal relationships. Golds might ask us to read biographies and case studies about "successful" people as examples of how sacrifice leads to success. They might insist that we study history to avoid repeating past mistakes. Greens might expect us to read about scientists and inventors. They might want us to study the scientific process as the primary tool for improving our quality of life. Finally, Oranges might want us to read about explorers and mountain climbers. They might expect us to study examples of how risk-takers have blazed trails that have forever changed our world.

f. What Mistake #6 Looks Like

Mistake #6, attempting to force others to believe and live as you do, is really the culmination of all the other mistakes. Blues want everyone to be more Blue. Blues think of themselves as non-judgmental. Yet, they have a problem with anyone who fails to express interest in and work toward improving human relationships. Golds know that they are judgmental. They simply don't see any reason to change. After all, who doesn't know right from wrong? Greens find it hard to imagine that everyone would not be better off with fewer prejudices and less of a reliance on emotions. They worship at the altar of objectivity. Oranges find most people lacking in any sense of adventure. They know that the world would be better off if people would just be more honest and direct with one another. And incidentally, a good Orange laugh each day would make everyone's life less stressful.

g. A Summary of the Six Mistakes

The interesting thing about Cicero's six mistakes is that they reaffirm what

Your Relationship Glass
Focusing on How Full Rather than How Empty

we have been saying about Colors throughout this book. Mistakes (liabilities) are simply strengths that we carry too far. Isn't it ironic that we can read these six mistakes and know that we are laughing at our own liabilities; yet, we have a difficult time changing our attitudes and behaviors?

Mistake #1   Thinking of life in terms of winners and losers

Mistake #2   Worrying about things over which you have little control

Mistake #3   Assuming that no answer exists because you don't know what it is

Mistake #4   Settling for what you know without considering what might be possible

Mistake #5   Failing to read and learn about new ideas

Mistake #6   Attempting to force others to believe and live as you do

Habits can be both good and bad. When they are good, we tend to take them for granted. When they are bad, we tend to ignore them – at least when they are our mistakes. Our menu may be somewhat limited, but we've grown accustomed to it. Let's turn our attention now to how we can change our habits by seeing the Relationship glass as half-full rather than half-empty.

Studying the Relationship Glass

In his book, *Emotional Intelligence*, Goleman (1995) indicates that what sets those at the very top of competitive pursuits apart from others of roughly equal ability is **enthusiasm** and **persistence**. How enthusiastic are you about developing positive relationships with other people? How

Your Relationship Glass
Focusing on How Full Rather than How Empty

persistent are you in thinking about and acting on those attitudes and behaviors that build healthy relationships?

Does it surprise you to know that if you work enthusiastically and persistently at relationships, you are more likely to achieve and sustain them? Is your attitude glass half empty or half full? Are you enthusiastic, optimistic, and persistent? Do you believe that you have the intellectual and emotional capacity to improve your personal relationships with others?

Like relationships, attitudes don't just happen. They are developed over time and are influenced by life experiences. Friends often say to me, *"I don't get that Colors stuff. You say I'm Green, but I don't act like Dave, and you say he's Green too."*

Again, no one is one Color. We are all a grand and glorious rainbow of Colors. However, some of us are more attuned to our Colors than others. Think about a particular relationship: with a colleague at work, a friend, or a spouse/significant other. How in tune are you to your colors? How in tune is your partner to his/her colors? How in tune are you to one another's colors? Do you focus on what you both bring to the relationship table or what is missing? Consider this question as you read the following disagreement between Remi and Kim.

Remi is an Orange/Blue newlywed. Her husband, Kim, is a Green/Orange. Remi works as a fashion designer. She travels a great deal and tends to get upset with Kim for forgetting when she will be in or out of town. Kim owns an auto-parts business but lives for weekends so that he can go to the

Your Relationship Glass

Focusing on How Full Rather than How Empty

NASCAR races. Kim gets very impatient with Remi if she isn't in town on a weekend so that she can go to the races with him. It seems to Kim that when he and Remi were first dating, they never missed a Saturday at the racetrack. Lately, however, she seems to be missing more and more races because of her business travel out of the country.

Their latest and most heated argument came last weekend when Remi was actually in town but insisted that she needed to work on a dress design rather than going to the racetrack. This argument had upset both of them, and they had actually gone three days without speaking to one another. On Wednesday evening they had made up over dinner and dancing followed by what they laughingly refer to as a passionate night of forgiveness. But Kim is actually beginning to worry about their relationship. He worries that Remi's career is already placing a strain on their marriage. He hopes they have more in common than dancing, racecars, and the normal passions of a newlywed couple?

Analyzing the Relationship Glass

Let's take a moment to analyze Remi and Kim's relationship glass. Figure 4.2 illustrates what each adds to the relationship glass in terms of primary and follow-up colors. They know how full their glass is. Notice that Remi and Kim's glass is three quarters full in terms of the four colors. The only color that they don't have in their relationship glass is gold. You might argue that they each have Gold if they could call on it, but it is not evident in their combined primary and follow-up colors (Orange/Blue and Green/Orange).

During their argument Kim accused Remi of being thoughtless for planning her business trip during the biggest NASCAR weekend of the summer. Remi responded that she had informed Kim about her trip six weeks earlier. Kim then responded that Remi had originally planned to leave on Sunday instead of Saturday. The argument ended as follows:

Remi and Kim's Relationship Glass
Figure 4.2

> *"I told you I'd try to get a flight on Sunday, and I did. But I couldn't get it."*
> (Green logic – thought but not spoken)

Your Relationship Glass
Focusing on How Full Rather than How Empty

"That's because you waited until the last minute to book your flight."
(Argumentative Orange – gotcha)

"I'm sorry! I was working until all hours trying to complete these designs. Then you insisted that we spend that week in the mountains with your parents. And besides, you didn't tell me that was the week-end of the big race." (It's your fault Blue – you don't appreciate how hard I work)

"I just can't see why it is always my fault. You know that the week with my parents was more business than vacation. Dad and I had those three days of meetings with our suppliers. And the race is the same weekend every summer. We've been going to it for four years now." (If it's the Blue game you want to play – I'm the one who has been thinking of others)

"Well, excuse me! I guess my dresses aren't as important as your parts suppliers! And I guess my memory isn't quite as magnificent as your memory!" (Let's do battle Orange – if this is about who is more wrong, it certainly can't be me)

Imagine increasing pitch and volume, tears, condescending tones, and slamming doors, and you can see why this argument ended in three days of silence. But what aspects of their combined colors from their relationship glass contributed to it? What missing aspects might have stood in the way of a quicker resolution to their disagreement? And what might Kim and Remi do in the future to avoid such conflicts?

Your Relationship Glass

Focusing on How Full Rather than How Empty

a. The Colors in the Relationship Glass

In *The Real Colors Homeowner's Guide* I introduced Bobby, a fifth grader, who said, "I get it; a liability is nothing more than a strength we carry too far." Sometimes we develop a strength to such an extent that we impede other areas of our personality. We are so busy functioning in our preferred Color that we forget to develop other Colors – use them or lose them. In times of stress and anger we tend to revert to what we know best, our primary color – including both its strengths and its liabilities.

In Kim and Remi's situation both the liabilities of their primary and follow-up colors (Orange, Blue, and Green) and the absence of Gold are evident in their argument. Kim started the argument through his Green logic by referring to what he characterized as Remi's failure to think (lack of Green). Initially Remi argued against Kim's logical and somewhat condescending analysis through her point-by-point, competitive Orange. Then when Kim's logic did not work, he upped the ante by pushing back from his Orange. As he pushed harder, Remi went into her Blue – first the true Blue "I'm sorry," and then the righteous indignation Blue "Well excuse me!" Kim then reverted to his Green – Why is it always my fault (translated, how could it be my fault given my incredible ability to be logical and precise)? Through it all, neither one dug deep enough to pull from their Gold. How many of Cicero's six mistakes have Remi and Kim committed thus far?

Neither Remi nor Kim had been very effective at employing their Gold. Kim had not reminded Remi of the race. With other things on her mind, Remi lost sight of the fact that her presence was actually part of the race for Kim. To Kim the race was not the race unless he and Remi shared it. Greens often fail to communicate their thoughts and intent. They fail to consider logistical needs. Remi had not purchased her ticket far enough in advance to get a Sunday flight instead of a Saturday flight. Oranges tend to get involved in so many tasks that they find themselves trying to take care of logistical details at the last minute.

Kim failed to recognize when his analysis had shifted to condemnation. Greens are sometimes oblivious to feeling cues. And when their "strategic planning" is called into question, they must defend their Green logical honor. Kim's Green logic and Orange competitiveness brought about his "I just can't see why it is always my fault," comment. Do you see any more examples of the six mistakes?

b. Let's Fix What Is Wrong

After making up, Kim and Remi decided that they needed to do a better job of organizing their time and communicating their plans to one another. They bought calendars, created to do lists that they posted on the refrigerator, and even tried to enlist Kim's secretary/bookkeeper, a Gold's Gold, in organizing and coordinating their schedules. They started moving to this Gold standard with great fanfare. They bought expensive and sophisticated day-timers and told friends and family about their intentions to become more organized. When Remi lost her day-timer, Kim was quietly but obviously disgusted with her. Realizing that he did not want to inflame her righteous indignation Blue again, Kim told Remi that they could both write their important information in his day-timer, and he would make certain that his secretary took care of any major scheduling conflicts.

As time went on, however, Kim found it more and more difficult to coordinate his calendar with his secretary's on a regular basis. Soon the impossible occurred – the date of her office party that Remi had entered in Kim's calendar never got to his secretary's calendar. When Kim failed to coordinate the two calendars, his secretary scheduled something else on that day. Can you predict the details of that argument?

Remi had forgotten to remind Kim of the office party on that Friday morning, and she had been unable to reach him on his cell phone all day. But she wasn't worried about Kim forgetting the party. After all, Mary (his secretary) had entered it on both calendars – or so Remi thought. Remi's only concern was that Kim might wait too long to leave the store and get caught in traffic. As her coworkers left the office for the restaurant, several had offered Remi a ride. But she explained that Kim was often late and would probably arrive any minute.

> *"He probably let his cell phone battery go dead again. He is always forgetting to charge it," she said. "We'll just be a few minutes late."*

When 6:00 came and went with no call from Kim, Remi called home. But there was no answer there. Hurt and angry, Remi called a cab, turned off her cell phone, and went to the party alone.

When Kim arrived home at 6:15, he assumed Remi was running late. After failing to reach her on her office phone or her cell phone, he became

Your Relationship Glass
Focusing on How Full Rather than How Empty

worried. He called the local hospital, checked with the police to see if Remi had been in an accident, and then got in his car and went to her office. He called several of Remi's friends from work but couldn't reach anyone. At 10:00 Kim returned home, and at 10:20 Remi walked through the door.

"Just where have you been?" he shouted.

Where have I been? You certainly have a lot of nerve asking me where I've been, mister," she slurred.

"You've been out drinking with your friends, haven't you?"

"I had a couple drinks after dinner. After all, thanks to you I needed to get a ride with Charlotte."

Remi and Kim eventually shouted their way to an understanding of what had happened. By that time they had damaged their normal communications pathways, committing all of Cicero's six mistakes. Remi had criticized Kim for forgetting to put the date of her office party on his secretary's calendar. Kim had reminded Remi that she had been the one to lose her calendar in the first place.

Remi and Kim meant well in trying to fix their common liability – a lack of Gold. But what they had done was to see their relationship glass as one-fourth empty rather than as three-fourths full. They had focused on their liability instead of focusing on their strengths. Can you think of a time when you have found yourself in a similar situation? Let's take a moment to see how they might have handled their problem differently.

c. Let's Focus on What We Do Well

Remi and Kim's relationship glass contained two parts Orange, one part
Blue, and one part Green — three of the four Colors available in any person's
rainbow. The only thing they lacked was an adequate amount of Gold, the
last color in both their Color rainbows. Unfortunately they had followed a
relationship *improvement* process rather than a relationship *renewal*
process. That is, they had attempted to fix what was missing from their
relationship rather than trying to build on what had brought them together
in the first place. Kim and Remi had been drawn to one another initially as
a result of their mutual lack of regard for Gold. Growing up, they had
become weary of their parents and teachers' admonitions for their lack of
Gold. As a young couple they had little reason to worry about their lack of
order and occasional tardiness. Remi had gone into fashion design because
it had fit her creative nature. Kim owned his own store because he wanted
the freedom to do things his own way. Remi's boss didn't care if she arrived
at work late as long as her designs were completed on time. Once Kim's
customers learned that he might be five or ten minutes late opening his
store, they simply made another stop before going to Kim's. And since
Kim would also be a few minutes late closing his store, they knew they
could get that late afternoon part at his store when every other auto parts
store would be closed.

But as Kim and Remi both became more successful in their work, they
found that their individual freedom had begun to conflict more and more
with their time together. They became focused on what was missing from
their glass instead of what was in it.

Your Relationship Glass
Focusing on How Full Rather than How Empty

You can learn to focus on what is in your Relationship glass rather than what is missing. Figure 4.3 illustrates how Kim and Remi analyzed their Relationship glass. The first column lists the Color questions that should have come to bear on this calendar issue. (Notice that the Gold question is in bold type, to indicate that the calendar is a Gold solution to the time commitment.) Column two illustrates whether the question falls naturally into either Kim or Remi's strengths – their primary or follow-up Colors. Column three asks whether or not Remi and Kim brought each of the four Color questions to bear in terms of their calendar challenge.

Remi and Kim both had Orange to apply in this situation, and they applied it. They took action by purchasing and using a day-timer. When Remi lost her day-timer, she wrote her commitments in Kim's calendar. Kim, in turn, wrote them into his secretary's calendar so that she could keep him on task. But let's look at how Remi failed to use her Blue and Kim failed to use his Green effectively.

It is not surprising that Remi and Kim failed to ask the Gold question: what does success look like to each of us based on our life-experiences? Gold, after all, is the last Color in both their Color rainbows. What is interesting, however, is that they failed to ask the Blue and Green questions. Remi had adequate Blue, her follow-up color, to force the Blue question: why is this time commitment issue important to us? Likewise, Kim had adequate Green, his primary color, to force the Green question: how can we adjust our individual expectations to meet our common goal (keeping our time commitments to one another)?

Your Relationship Glass

Focusing on How Full Rather than How Empty

Drinking From Your Relationship Glass

Figure 4.3

Question	Is the Color Readily Available?	Was the Color Question Adequately Pursued?
Blue Why is this time commitment issue important to Remi and to Kim?	Yes – Remi	No
Gold What does success look like to each of them based on their life experiences?	No	No
Green How can they adjust their individual expectations to meet their common goals?	Yes – Kim	No
Orange Where do they start to ensure the greatest likelihood of renewing their relationship?	Yes – Both Remi and Kim	Yes

Focusing on your strengths does not mean you can ignore a deficit. In every situation it is important to ask all four of the Color questions. Then as you examine your answers, you can decide where you will need the least advice from another source – those areas where you have the most ability. In addition, you can be much more specific in asking help from others. Figure 4.4 – shown on the next page – illustrates how this process can work.

But it helps when both parties to the relationship share a common commitment to one another, a commitment that transcends personal gain. If you work enthusiastically and persistently at relationships, you are more

An Assets Refinement Model

Figure 4.4

Question	Answer	Action
Blue Why is this time commitment issue important to Remi and to Kim?	Since their relationship cup contains a lot of Orange, they need a way to coordinate their individual schedules to make the most of their time together.	Since Kim is not a romantic, Remi could place special little love messages reminding him two or three times each week of an important upcoming event: in his wallet, on his voice mail, on the refrigerator, etc.
Gold What does success look like to each of them based on their life experiences?	They would schedule important events that they wanted to share together – particularly on weekends.	Once Kim and Remi plan their strategies in other areas, they may ask a Gold friend to analyze it for gaps. (Know where to ask for help and what specific help you want.)
Green How can they adjust their individual expectations to meet their common goals?	Since Gold is the last color in their rainbows, they should probably plan for multiple safety guards or reminders of important events.	Kim can create a schedule for their reminders and a plan for them to check-in with each other on a regular basis. He might schedule the time for them to
Orange Where do they start to ensure the greatest likelihood of renewing their relationship?	Since they are both fun loving and hate routines, they could plan creative reminders and try to place them in unique places for one another.	Kim and Remi could place friendly bets on who could come up with the most (or the most original) reminders of important events. To avoid setting the competition stakes too high, they might put their individual winnings into a piggybank to be used for a nice dinner as a reward for helping one another become more organized.

Your Relationship Glass

Focusing on How Full Rather than How Empty

likely to achieve and sustain them. When you learn to see your Relationship glass as half-full rather than half-empty, you focus on your mutual strengths. You use what you have as a means of filling in the gaps in terms of your missing colors. When you are enthusiastic, optimistic, and persistent about recognizing your common interests and strengths, you will take the time to gain a deeper understanding of those strengths in action. But without a commitment to a purpose that is greater than either partner's individual satisfaction, it will be difficult to sustain a successful relationship over time.

Before we consider how to sustain a strong and vibrant relationship, take a moment to respond to the items on the next few pages. As you do, ask yourself how enthusiastic and persistent you are in the pursuit of meaningful relationships.

Analyzing Your Relationships Glass

1. Choose a relationship and use it to fill your relationship glass. (Use your combined primary and follow-up colors.)

2. What colors do you and your partner bring to the relationship? Are any of these colors common to both of you? What color(s) are missing from your glass?

3. Take a specific disagreement that has occurred recently involving you and a relationship partner and analyze which of Cicero's six mistakes you made. Give examples of mistakes made by both you and your partner.

**My Relationships
Glass**

Your Relationship Glass
Focusing on How Full Rather than How Empty

Mistake #1   An illusion that personal gain is realized by crushing others

Me	My partner

Mistake #2   A tendency to worry about those things that cannot be changed or corrected

Me	My partner

Your Relationship Glass
Focusing on How Full Rather than How Empty

Mistake #3   An insistence that things are impossible because we
cannot achieve them

Me	My partner

Mistake #4   A refusal to set aside trivial preferences

Me	My partner

Mistake #5   A failure to develop our minds through the habits of reading and study

Me	My partner

Mistake #6   An attempt to compel others to believe and live as we do

Me	My partner

Your Relationship Glass

Focusing on How Full Rather than How Empty

4. Use the chart below to analyze how you might renew your relationship by seeing your glass as half-full.

Question	Answer	Action
Blue Why is this relationship important to my partner and me?		
Gold What does success look like to each of us based on our life experiences?		
Green How can we adjust our individual expectations to meet our commitments to one another?		
Orange Where do we start to ensure the greatest likelihood of renewing our relationship?		

Growing
Your Own
Food

Growing Your Own Food

Most of us spend our lives eating food that someone else has prepared. Some more adventurous souls play with recipes or prepare their meals according to the recipes they have learned from parents, teachers, and mentors. As we have discussed from a Colors perspective throughout this book, this means that to a great extent our attitudes and beliefs are simply a reflection of other people's thinking and experiences.

The purpose of this chapter is to show you how to take responsibility for your own relationships. This is not the starting point of relationship building. It is a threshold to a new level in your relationships. To get started, ask yourself, **"What kind of relationship do I want to create, and what will I do with it once I have created it?"**

So far, we have considered what a Real relationship looks like, what questions you need to ask as you begin a relationship, what habits you need to develop to sustain a healthy relationship, and how you can focus on what works for you and your relationship partner. Now that you have had a chance to practice the fundamentals of relationship building, let's turn our attention to making these skills your own. Take a moment to focus on a relationship that is important to you and ask yourself the following questions:

- *How are the admonitions (pruning) that parents, teachers, and mentors used to shape my growth affecting my relationship habits today?*

- *How are the accolades (fertilizers) that parents, teachers, and mentors used to shape my growth affecting my relationship habits today?*

• *Am I now comfortable enough with this partner that we could consider reshaping our relationship habits?*

The Effects of Pruning on Relationship Building

I cannot remind you often enough that your relationships with other people are a result of who the two of you have become as individuals. In the Homeowner's Guide we talked about the "stuff" that people collect as a result of their Colors. Figure 5.1 presents concrete examples of stuff that people of varying Colors might naturally collect. Remember, these are illustrative rather than absolute examples of your Color stuff.

Where's My Stuff
Figure 5.1

Blue		Green	
Art	Old birthday cards	Computer	Birdwatcher's guide
CD's	Telephone	Computer games	Fax
Old love notes	Fireplace	Science magazines	Puzzle books
Poetry	Dream catchers	Telescope	Stereo headphones
Gold		Orange	
File cabinet	Bookcase	Tennis racket	Big screen television
Table	Pencil sharpener	Golf clubs	Joke books
Rolodex	Notepad	Keys to motorcycle	Snack food
Snack tray	Dictionary	Sports Illustrated	Games

Source: Real Colors Homeowner's Guide

What is your Color order – which Color is most like you, next, next, and least? If you are Blue, your primary focus is on connections among human beings and concepts that transcend physical or scientific explanations. If you are Gold, you focus primarily on concrete, day-to-day objects and events and how they fit into established manageable categories. If you are Green, you focus primarily on underlying connections among ideas and principles that affect your life over time. If you are Orange, you focus primarily on concrete objects and events that are most readily available and hold the greatest potential to bring about what you want now.

When you were a small child, numerous adults shaped your life. During your preschool years this included primarily parents and close relatives. When you reached school age, you were influenced by teachers and coaches. Then in adolescence your peers became increasingly influential in shaping your attitudes and beliefs. Usually with the best of intentions all these individuals tried to prune some of your attitudes and beliefs that they felt might be detrimental to your personal development. Let's consider what some of this developmental pruning might have looked in terms of each Color.

Figures 5.2 and 5.3 illustrate why adults might try to prune potential liabilities in a young person. In each figure I've limited the examples to three for each Color, but you can extend the charts with your own examples. Figure 5.2 focuses on pruning for abstract branches. Figure 5.3 focuses on pruning for concrete branches. To understand these pruning tendencies, you need to think first about the strengths related to each Color. Then consider how those strengths might become liabilities if they are carried too far. Finally, think about why adult caregivers might want to prune these liabilities in order to "shape" a young person in positive ways.

Pruning to Control Abstract Liabilities
Figure 5.2

Blue	Green
Strength	
Care giver	Logical
Able to express emotions openly	Planner
Peacemaker	Precise
Liability	
Easily taken advantage of	Aloof
Easily hurt	Procrastinator
Easily manipulated	Fault finder
Reason for Pruning	
Gold: Learn to stand on your own two feet before you try to help someone else Gentle people need to be toughened up to avoid being hurt You have to stand for something **Green:** In the real world you can't save everyone All that emotion stuff can interfere with a person's judgment Peace and harmony should not be gained at the expense of logic and integrity **Orange:** Life's too short to worry about everyone else's problems Emotional people miss too much fun by worrying about everyone else's feelings Competition is a necessary part of life	**Blue:** People are more important than ideas People don't care how much you know until they know how much you care It's more important to be human than to be right **Gold:** People need to be good team players The road to hell is paved with good intentions It's easy to complain from the sidelines **Orange:** People can't stand a know-it-all While some people plan, the rest of us are doing the work If you wait for everything to be perfect, nothing will ever get done

of the branches listed in the third column? Or are you a concrete —
Gold or Orange? In that case, ask yourself the same questions relative to
the chart below.

Pruning to Control Potential Concrete Liabilities
Figure 5.3

Gold	Orange
Strength	
Reliable/predictable	Fun loving
Loyal	Risk taker
Thrifty	Open to new ideas
Liability	
Boring	Childish
Follower	Careless
Tightwad	Unpredictable
Reason for Pruning	
Blue: Caring human beings know how to be flexible People should follow their dreams Wealth is not as important as friendships	**Blue:** They care more about fun than about people's feelings They care more about doing than being People need to think about how their actions affect others
Green: Reliability is only useful when you are reliably correct Integrity is more important than loyalty Sometimes it takes a little more money to do things right	**Gold:** Responsibilities come before fun It seems a waste to risk a lifetime of work on a whim
Orange: Variety is the spice of life	**Green:** Reliability is only useful when you are reliably correct Integrity is more important than loyalty Sometimes it takes a little more money to do things right

allowing the roots to support more berries in the future. Although you should not ignore or "pluck" the blossoms from a new relationship, you do need to remember that relationships require strong roots if they are going to flourish over time. They need to be "rooted" in your common values. Remember, appropriate care for new plants differs depending on soil conditions, amount of water, other plants in the area, etc. Likewise, relationships require different kinds of care and nurturing depending on each individual's past experiences, aspirations, and willingness to take risks.

Parents, family members, and early acquaintances have a tremendous impact on our sense of relationships. Your parents used pruning to discourage what they thought could become your bad habits. As you grew, they expanded this pruning to include relationships. They wanted to protect you from becoming susceptible to the wrong crowd. *"I don't want you going to that party at John's house. I don't know his parents, and I've heard some questionable stories about John from several people at Rotary."*

Rosa was a Green-Orange child born to parents who were in their mid-forties. Rosa's birth was not unplanned. In fact, her mother wanted to have a fourth child in the hopes that this time she would have a little girl. Rosa's mother had been a 4-H sponsor and had visions of doing all those "girl things" with her own daughter. But Rosa's temperament, somewhat encouraged by her three older brothers, leaned more toward science and sports than toward 4-H and more traditional "girl things."

Rosa often went to baseball practice with her brothers. She loved football and would have played that too if she had been allowed. But Rosa was growing up prior to Title IX laws that provided opportunities for girls to play sports. By the time she reached adolescence, Rosa's sports and tomboy antics were no longer as funny to her parents or her older brothers as they had been when she was younger. Her father expected her to do farm

chores, but he admonished her for her "inappropriate" behaviors in social situations. Her brothers still liked to throw a football to their teenage sister, but they frequently questioned why their mother allowed Rosa to be so rude and "out of sync" with other girls her age. Rosa did not date in high school and did not fit into most of the "expected" activities for girls.

Rosa has been shaped by her parents' pruning, and she has found it difficult to take her own shape as an adult. Now in her middle age, Rosa is a single adult who still enjoys football more than a play. She has wrestled with her weight since her mid-twenties, and she still favors a football jersey to a blouse.

The shape of Rosa's early years did not only come through pruning, however. Her parents and older brothers also established individual and relationship expectations in the form of fertilizers or positive reinforcements of certain behaviors. Let's take a look at how these behavior fertilizers affected her.

The Effects of Fertilizers on Relationship Building

Rosa's father was also a Green-Orange. Her mother was a Blue-Gold. But Rosa's father was the dominant – in fact, overpowering – force in Rosa's family. Rosa's father was somewhat of a non-conformist at heart, but he was raised with traditional values that caused his Green questioning and Orange sense of adventure to be limited. He admired Rosa's free spirit as long as it didn't collide with his own. Steeped in the Calvinist idea of hard work, Rosa's father expected all of his children to be responsible for numerous farm chores. When Rosa's mother complained about Rosa's lack of social graces, her father would say, "Well, she's your daughter. Why don't you keep her in the house and make her work on in-door chores?"

How much are Rosa's personal attitudes and behaviors a result of her parents' pruning and fertilizers? There is no way to know for certain, but let's consider what can happen when parents and other adult caregivers over-fertilize to encourage certain behaviors. Figures 5.4 and 5.5 indicate how adults might encourage potential liabilities in a young person by over-fertilizing. As with the pruning charts, I've limited the examples to three for each Color. Again, you can extend the charts with your own examples. But notice that in column three of the charts the fertilizer is being added by an adult of the same Color. That is, the adult is encouraging the further development of a natural behavior or attitude for the child in column one. Figure 5.4 focuses on fertilizers that could create abstract liabilities. Figure 5.5 focuses on fertilizers that risk creating concrete liabilities.

The statements in column three are positive reinforcements of the strengths listed in column one. They build a sense of self-confidence. But as you saw from Rosa's example above, they can also reinforce the liabilities within any color.

Are you an abstract – a Blue or a Green? Did you have a parent, grandparent, or teacher who fertilized your behavior in ways similar to the statements listed in the third column? Although these fertilizers worked at the time, have they caused you to develop behaviors and attitudes that have eventually become a liability for you?

The Side-Effects of Over-Fertilizing Abstract Characteristics
Figure 5.4

Blue	Green
Strength	
Care giver Able to express emotions openly Peacemaker	Logical Planner Precise
Liability	
Easily taken advantage of Easily hurt Easily manipulated	Aloof Procrastinator Fault finder
Reasons for Using Fertilizers	
Blue: It's better to have loved and lost than to never have loved at all Don't give up your dreams Other people simply don't understand sensitive people like you and me	**Green:** It is far more important to be respected than to be popular It's better to do one thing right than to do several things half-way I think this is a great start, but is it your best effort?

When you are surrounded by adults and older siblings who encourage and reward your behaviors and attitudes, you can eventually "carry your strengths too far." You may begin to clutter the other three rooms of your Color home with your Blue or Green stuff. When you do that, you impair your ability to function effectively in your other Colors, and this can impede your ability to form effective relationships with other people.

The Side-Effects of Over-Fertilizing Concrete Characteristics
Figure 5.5

Gold	Orange
Strength	
Reliable/predictable	Fun loving
Loyal	Risk taker
Thrifty	Open to new ideas
Liability	
Boring	Childish
Follower	Careless
Tightwad	Unpredictable
Reasons for Using Fertilizers	
Gold: It's better to be safe than to be sorry.	**Orange:** I'm glad you're not one of those stuffed-shirt intellectuals.
It's important to be a team player.	A mistake is just one more learning experience.
You can't help other people if you don't take care of your own basic needs.	Life is an adventure; live it to the fullest.

Let's see how this same phenomenon applies to a concrete Gold or Orange? What are the potential liabilities of over-fertilizing concrete behaviors and attitudes?

Which chart includes your primary color? Did you have adults around you as you were growing up who encouraged those behaviors – fertilized them?

Did they over-fertilize those behaviors to a point that you now expect every-one to "appreciate who you are?"

Most parents want to create the ideal family. They want to do all those things that their parents (regardless of how attentive they may have been) just didn't quite understand or have the time to do. Or in some cases, they want to do everything "exactly as mom and dad did for them". While either of these approaches has merit, both are reactions to what was. They lack a consideration of what is and what might be. Think about Rosa, whose parents, you might say, reinforced nontraditional behaviors for a girl. Perhaps they sent Rosa mixed messages. But what about Jake and Hauney from chapter three.

Jake's parents were educators. His mother was a stay at home mom until Jake's younger sister went to junior high school. His mother's sole reason to exist seemed to be to make Jake and his sister's life meaningful. She sang in the church choir, hauled the kids to dance lessons and football practice, and nightly tucked "her babies" into bed.

That's what Jake was looking for in a relationship. He was resigned to his wife's working part time after the children were born. But he expected to find a partner who would place family above career so that his children could know the love and stability he had known as a child.

Hauney, on the other hand, was a successful attorney who was adopted by a middle-aged couple. Hauney was the center of her parents' lives, an only child who was bright and outgoing. Both her parents were able to rearrange their schedules to attend Hauney's dance recitals, her gymnastics competitions, and every parent conference including parents' weekends in college. Hauney could not imagine sitting at home while her husband took care of her and the family. She could not picture herself as a room mother or a PTA president.

Jake and Hauney are a typical example of two people who seem to have a great deal in common. Neither was abused nor neglected. Neither was sent mixed messages about their parents' expectations. But each one learned a slightly different recipe for achieving a happy, stable, and loving home life. Have you thought about the pruning and fertilizers that the adults in your life used to shape who you have become? In the Homeowner's Guide you considered how you could take an inventory of your Color stuff. Have you taken that inventory? Are you ready now to take a similar inventory with a relationship partner? It is not enough to ask another person what they value. You need to ask them what that value looks like in action. You have to grow your own sense of who you are as individuals and what you want to become as a result of your relationship with one another.

Organic Relationship Gardening

A relationship is organic. It grows and changes. What you need to decide is the extent to which you are committed to helping one another grow. If you want to gain the most from a relationship, it needs to be grounded in **Real Colors**® principles. It needs to be organic. Partners in a **Real Colors**-based relationship have to learn to understand who they are individually and as a partnership. You can use the Four-P questions to grow an organic relationship without over pruning or fertilizing.

Purpose	Why is this important to you and to me?
Parameters	What does it look like to each of us based on our life experiences?
Principles	How can we adjust our individual expectations from the past to accommodate the realities of our life today?
Priorities	Where do we start to ensure the greatest likelihood of building a relationship that is meaningful and fulfilling to both of us?

Each member of the relationship must feel free to risk answering these questions. It may be healthy to explore with one another how past pruning and fertilizing may still be driving your expectations. Are you a Blue who was over-fertilized and now may not have realistic expectations for your partner? Or are your expectations of one another a result of seeking something that was not there in your earlier life experiences? In other words, do you have unrealistic expectations of one another now to make up for past pruning?

While it is important to recognize and understand the significance of past pruning and fertilizers, it is equally important to avoid dwelling on them. You don't want to relive past problems or use them as excuses for not getting on with your life and with this relationship. But at the same time, you should not expect yourself or your relationship partner to create an organic relationship overnight. People use pruning and fertilizers because they get results. Have you ever tried to prune or fertilize your partner to create the ideal relationship? Take a look at Figure 5.6 to see what message(s) you are sending to your partner?

Relationship Pruning and Fertilizing

Figure 5.6

Pruning and Fertilizers	Potential Message
Blue	
Pruning – Why can't you understand how that makes me feel?	You need to make me happy.
Fertilizer – I would do anything to make you happy.	I'll take total responsibility for this aspect of our relationship.
Gold	
Pruning – Why can't you be more organized?	You are such a klutz.
Fertilizer – I should have reminded you of that this morning.	I'll assume the guilt and responsibility for your mistake.
Green	
Pruning – The car looks great, but why didn't you clean the windows?	You don't care enough to do it right?
Fertilizer – I don't know why I can't be more helpful to you in these situations.	I am so bright that I need to remember to do everything to make this relationship work.
Orange	
Pruning – Why are you always so anal-retentive?	Your organization is getting in the way of my fun.
Fertilizer – I'll plan a really exciting trip for us.	You wouldn't know how to plan an exciting trip.

Obviously you cannot be certain how a partner is going to interpret your words and gestures. You might also question the strength of your relationship if you need to measure every word. The important thing to remember is that you take for granted that other people understand the intent of your words. The more you and your relationship partner discuss past experiences and explain why certain words or gestures have a negative impact on you, the more likely you can avoid offending one another through words or through body language. If you don't have such discussions, you cannot grow your relationship. But how do you know when you are being over- or under-sensitive?

There is no magic sensitivity standard. But contrary to the pop-culture response to being "politically correct," there is a balance between taking all the responsibility for the success of a relationship and taking no responsibility whatsoever. A Real relationship is not built on politics. Political solutions come about when people don't feel that they have enough in common to seek a synergistic solution to a problem. "I will give you what you want so that you will leave me alone." Or, "I'll give you something you want now so that I can get you to do something I want you to do later." Such solutions to a relationship dilemma constitute parallel play – having someone else in the room for company without depending on or making commitments to one another.

Covey (1989) talks about the need to build an emotional bank account in any relationship. "I am someone you can trust to care about you, to listen to you, and to honor your beliefs as well as your privacy." When you and your partner add to this bank account assuming that it belongs to both of you, you grow your relationship. When you carry separate accounts and keep track of your debts to one another, you create a business agreement. Figure 5.7 illustrates how you can build a Real reservoir of good will that not only sustains but grows your relationships.

Growing An Organic Relationship
Figure 5.7

from Pruning and Fertilizers	to Organic
Blue	
Pruning – Why can't you understand how that makes me feel? ***Fertilizer*** – I would do anything to make you happy.	I know you didn't mean to upset me this morning, but I need to tell you how your comment affected me. I also need to recognize if there was something I said that may have triggered your response.
Gold	
Pruning – Why can't you be more organized? ***Fertilizer*** – I should have reminded you of that this morning.	I probably worry too much about being organized, but I must find some ways to meet my need for structure without destroying the sensitivity (logic/flexibility) that you bring to our relationship.
Green	
Pruning – The car looks great, but why didn't you clean the windows? ***Fertilizer*** – I don't know why I can't be more helpful to you in these situations.	Come out here and look at the car windows. I was so impressed with your car wash that I wanted to get some attention too.
Orange	
Pruning – Why are you always so anal-retentive? ***Fertilizer*** – I'll plan a really exciting trip for us.	There are several things we've talked about doing on our next vacation. How about if I make a list of them and then you can figure out what we really have time to do?

Growing Your Own Food

There are several things we've talked about doing on our next vacation. How about if I make a list of them and then you can figure out what we really have time to do?

Again, a Real relationship depends on more than a series of political tradeoffs. Notice that the statements in the organic column are neither accusatory nor apologetic. The Gold example provides options (sensitivity, logic, flexibility) that can be directed from a Gold to a Blue, Green, or Orange respectively. The Green example just below the Gold illustrates the value of some slightly self-deprecating humor in communicating a desire to meet both your own and your partner's needs within the relationship. The Orange example illustrates that you can recognize directly what each of you brings to the table within your relationship. The important thing to remember is to strive for balance and mutual respect. The words themselves become secondary when both members of the relationship try to be more sensitive to issues of intent.

As a school superintendent, I am often frustrated by people's assumptions about communications. "We need to improve communications around here." OR "I think we simply had a communications breakdown." Communications involve more than speaking or listening. They involve more than words and messages. Real communications occur on three levels as illustrated in Figure 5.8.

Real Communications
Figure 5.8

In the next chapter we will consider how levels of intimacy affect and are affected by the amount of effort two people are willing to put into a relationship. But first, take a moment to sharpen your organic gardening skills by responding to the items on the next few pages. How ready are you and partner to grow your own food that will take your relationship to the next level?

Growing Your Relationship

(You may find it most helpful for you and your partner to complete most of the following items separately and then to discuss your responses together.)

1. In the chart below write *Me* in the cell that describes your primary
    Color and me in the cell that represents your follow-up or secondary
    Color. Then write *My Partner* in the cell that describes your partner's
    primary Color and *My Partner* in the cell that represents your partner's
    follow-up or secondary Color.

Where's Our Stuff

Blue		Green	
Art	Old birthday cards	Computer	Birdwatcher's guide
CD's	Telephone	Computer games	Fax
Old love notes	Fireplace	Science magazines	Puzzle books
Poetry	Dream catchers	Telescope	Stereo headphones
Gold		**Orange**	
File cabinet	Bookcase	Tennis racket	Big screen television
Table	Pencil sharpener	Golf clubs	Joke books
Rolodex	Notepad	Keys to motorcycle	Snack food
Snack tray	Dictionary	Sports Illustrated	Games

2. What Color(s) do you have in common and what Color(s) are not
    primary or secondary to either of you?

3. What are the implications of this match for your relationship?

Relationship Strengths	Relationship Liabilities

4. Use the chart on the next page to list the effects of your own and your partner's past pruning and fertilizers.

5. Use the chart on page 131 to plan how you and your partner can move from Pruning and artificial Fertilizers to organic gardening. Use the entries from number four to fill in the first column.

6. How effectively do you and your partner communicate your individual needs within your relationship? What are your plans for taking communications and your overall relationship?

Relationship Pruning and Fertilizers

My Pruning and Fertilizers	My Partner's Pruning and Fertilizers
Blue	
Pruning –	
Fertilizers –	
Gold	
Pruning –	
Fertilizers –	
Green	
Pruning –	
Fertilizers –	
Orange	
Pruning –	
Fertilizers –	

Growing An Organic Relationship

From Pruning and Fertilizers	To Organic
Blue	

Pruning –

Fertilizers –

Gold	

Pruning –

Fertilizers –

Green	

Pruning –

Fertilizers –

Orange	

Pruning –

Fertilizers –

Growing Your Own Food

Entertaining:
Casual To
Candlelight

Entertaining: Casual To Candlelight

Once you start to grow your own relationship food, you become more aware of just how much human beings need one another. Organic relationship building involves two people moving beyond trying to shape one another. It involves a deeper level of understanding. Organic gardeners want to know the natural tendencies of different plants. They want to know how various plants interact with one another. They want to promote growth rather than stifling characteristics that they don't like or promoting the characteristics that they prefer. Organic gardeners want to understand the plants they grow so that they know how they react to and interact with one another.

The purpose of this chapter is to help you determine how much time and effort you are willing to invest in various relationships. As Robert Quinn (1996) suggests, "Deep change is an extensive learning process." It is never ending. But there are only so many hours in a day. There are only so many relationships that you will have time to develop in depth.

Stephen Montgomery writes a great deal about relationships. In his series of books on the *Pygmalion Project* (1989) and in his book *People Patterns* (2002) Montgomery describes how people of various temperaments try to shape other people's lives as well as how they may be susceptible to manipulation by other people. In relationships we are all susceptible to risk. The question is what risks you believe to be worth taking. Where do you want to put your efforts?

Figure 6.1 provides a way for you to consider relationships in terms of personal risk versus personal gain. For example, it may be easier (less of a risk) to practice your relationship skills on casual acquaintances. My wife frequently says, "What makes the difference? I'll never see that person again anyhow." On the other hand, if the other person is a casual acquaintance, you don't have the advantage of knowing their motivations, and you may not have an opportunity to get a great deal of feedback from them for future use. Your boss is an example of a person you need but who does not need you. This relationship could have a high payoff for you, but it may not be the place to start practicing your relationship skills. Children are examples of people with whom you don't want to begin practicing relationship skills. Your future (other than the choice of your nursing home) does not depend on them, but their future certainly depends on how you shape your relationship with them.

One of the least risky/high payoff relationships in the long-term is found with friends and marriage partners. These are people with whom you share a common commitment. If you are married, it can be both fun and rewarding to practice your relationship skills by focusing on building friendships with other couples. If you are not married, you may find it less stressful to practice relationship building skills with a friend. Take a moment to consider this point as it is illustrated in Figure 6.1.

Risk Versus Gain
Figure 6.1

		Personal Gain	
		Low	**High**
Personal Risk	**Low**	Casual acquaintances	People who share a common commitment
	High	People that need you but whom you don't need	People that you need but who don't need you

Entertaining: Casual To Candlelight

People who already share a common commitment (friendship or marriage) have a great deal to gain by practicing their relationship skills together. You are typically more willing to make mistakes in front of friends and family than you are in front of people that you don't know or that you depend on for your day-to-day survival. Let's begin by thinking about this safer level of practice – what I call casual entertainment.

Casual Entertainment

Face it. You will accomplish much more by practicing something you enjoy than by practicing something that is a drudgery. Since you've gotten this far in the book, you obviously see the benefits of developing your "relationship" skills. Make certain that this practice brings you joy. Mahaly Csikszentmihalyi (1990) suggests that enjoyment (or what he calls flow) requires eight components. Here is Csikszentmihalyi's recipe:

1. *Confront a challenging task that you have a chance of completing.*
2. *Concentrate on what you are doing.*
3. *Set clear goals.*
4. *Make certain that you have a way to get feedback.*
5. *Practice on something that is not a part of your daily responsibilities.*
6. *Make certain that you have control over your own actions.*
7. *Let go of self-conscious fears that may prevent you from reaching a higher level of consciousness.*
8. *Set aside time for practice; time passes quickly when you lose yourself in a task.*

Source: *Flow*, p. 49

1. Confront a challenging task that you have a chance of completing.

Relationships don't expand your experience if you stick to one temperament when you choose friends. In fact, while single Color relationships (Blue with Blue, Gold with Gold, etc.) are sometimes easier to initiate, they can soon become negative or pessimistic. For example, finish the sentence below with the first word that comes to your mind.

"I don't know why people can't be more…"

Did you say something like **considerate – Blue**? Did you say something like **responsible – Gold**? Was your response something like **reasonable – Green**? Or did you say **open – Orange**? When you surround yourself with people who think as you think or act as you act, you run the risk of reinforcing what you believe and wondering aloud with your partners why the rest of the world doesn't get it. School teachers wonder why people don't seem to care more about education. Accountants wonder why people aren't more precise with their budgets. My technology savvy son and his colleagues wonder why anyone would risk banking on-line.

Getting outside the box does not mean putting a different frosting on the same white cake. Try baking a pie. It's still a dessert, but it tests your skills. If you are Blue, get to know a Green. Don't pick a Green who believes that everything she does is right. Pick one who, like you, wants to grow. You might both be surprised at how much you can help one another grow.

2. Concentrate on what you are doing.

Remember, you are trying to expand your relationships. Don't expect to like everything about the other person at first. And be willing to suspend judgments. Ask the other person lots of questions, especially the Four-P questions.

Purpose	Why is that important to you?
Parameters	What does it look like — how would I know it if I saw it?
Principles	What other examples can you give me so that I can make it suit my needs?
Priorities	Where would I start if I wanted to learn to do that?

You are trying to understand another Color, not become that Color. Be who you are, but throw yourself into doing the other Color as a means of understanding its value to your partner and to yourself.

3. Set clear goals.

If you are Gold, you may say to yourself, *"I want to learn to do Orange so that I can relax and have a good time and so that others will realize that I can have a good time."* Then ask yourself what you would be doing if you were acting more Orange. What would Orange people be doing around you? What might people who know you say about the "new" you?

When you are attempting to grow as a person, you need to know what you want that growth to accomplish. You also need to let the person you are working with know what you want and what your level of comfort is with the impending change in your life. You need to set the target for change and decide when you feel comfortable enough to move it to the next level of challenge.

You also need to know what the other person wants from you. Don't try to tell them about your color. Start by asking them what they want to know. This will not only make it easier for you to help them do your color. It will renew your faith in yourself. You may be surprised how much other people admire what you take for granted about your temperament. On the other hand, don't get carried away with your answers or you may risk boring them and losing your gardener. Organic gardeners are rare. Don't risk losing one because you insist on protecting yourself with pesticides or adding self-serving, inorganic fertilizers to your food source.

4. Make certain that you have a way to get feedback.

When you grow an organic relationship, you don't have a formula or recipe. Deep change is a continuous learning process, and learning requires feedback. When you choose someone who can help you expand your relationship skill base, you need to agree on how you will provide one another feedback. You may want to discuss how each of you views criticism. How do you give it, and how do you take it? A spoonful of sugar helps the medicine go down. A cup full of sugar might make the medicine hard to swallow.

Accepting judgments is difficult for most people regardless of their Color. Limit the amount of feedback and make it specific to the goal or task at hand. Think about what will make the feedback most useful and least threatening for each partner. Suspending judgments is difficult for a Gold. Vague feedback is difficult for a Green. Feedback that fails to separate the action from the person can be devastating to a Blue. And feedback that fails to recognize the uniqueness of a solution will frustrate an Orange.

5. Practice on something that is not a part of your daily responsibilities.

When you invite a person to dinner, you probably won't try a series of new recipes. But you can mix a new dessert recipe with some familiar entrees. Likewise, don't try to expand your relationship skill set in a high stakes situation, for example, when your job depends on it. You will also feel more comfortable practicing a skill when you know that your partner is learning it with you. Challenge is good. Stress risks what Hart (1983) calls downshifting or avoidance behaviors.

You need to concentrate on your goal of relationship building. You need to do this in a situation that allows you to focus on growth – long term rather than short-term results. You need a safe environment to practice and a willingness to laugh at yourself. Covey (1989) tells us to begin with the end in mind, but he also reminds us to sharpen the saw – to take time for ourselves. This is a never ending journey. Don't confuse it with your daily tasks.

6. Make certain that you have control over your own actions.

If your partner tells you every step to take, you risk becoming dependent on his or her experience base. Again, ask questions. Why does your partner do something a particular way? Is this a pattern of his/her Color? Is it the result of pruning or residue from fertilizer? Or is it a one-time phenomenon? What are the underlying principles that will allow you to transfer your learning to new situations?

It is also important that you are growing your relationship skills because you want to grow them, not because someone else wants you to change. It is harder to sustain a change that is externally motivated than one that is internally motivated. It also takes patience to ride out the lulls and frustrations of a change process when you are personally committed to your goals.

7. Let go of self-conscious fears that may prevent you from reaching a higher level of consciousness.

Can you laugh at yourself? If you baked a cake for company and it flopped, could you serve it anyhow? Risk taking is not easy for most people. Oranges do better than most other Colors because they see mistakes as learning experiences. Greens often avoid situations unless they feel certain that they have the skills necessary to "pull it off." This is why you need to partner with someone who is willing to grow with you and to suspend judgments.

There is no better joy than achieving a goal that makes you stretch. Piaget (1952) called this cognitive dissonance. Others call it motivation. How many times did Edison fail before he invented the light bulb? How many baskets did Michael Jordan miss during those years that the Chicago Bulls won the national title? Look at mistakes as learning opportunities by analyzing what worked and what didn't, what surprised you, and how conditions may have varied from one experience to another.

8. Set aside time for practice; it passes quickly when you lose yourself in a task.

You will know that you are enjoying a task when two hours seem like ten minutes. When was the last time that you lost yourself completely in a task? What was it? Why did it captivate you? How did you feel when it was over?

When people believe that they have the skills to accomplish a task and they find that task challenging and personally interesting, they will stick with it. Make certain that you and your gardening partner share more than a willingness to practice. You will be more likely to practice regularly when you know and value what you expect as a result from that practice. Set goals and be certain to provide rewards for one another along the way.

Entertaining: Casual To Candlelight

Before we turn our attention to the higher stakes growth of candlelight dining, let's explore an example of casual dining. Clarke is a Green/Orange. His wife, Sally, is a Blue/Orange. Clarke and Sally decided that to expand their color repertoire they would get to know their Gold friends, Dan and Gloria.

At lunch one afternoon Sally told Gloria about **Real Colors**® and invited Gloria and Dan to join Clarke and her for dinner. After dinner Clarke and Sally talked with Dan and Gloria about Real Colors and gave them a copy of the *Homeowner's Guide*. The next week the two couples decided to grow their Color gardens together. They attended a **Real Colors** workshop and used this experience as a springboard to talk about their childhoods, being certain to share examples of how they had been pruned and fertilized. Clarke suggested that each of the four partners should take time to write down the examples of pruning and fertilizers from their past. They spent two or three hours discussing them.

Dan had been a Gold raised in a Gold home. He said he had so much fertilizer that he thought he'd choke on it. *"I was the mayor's son, captain of the football team, and homecoming king,"* Dan told them. *"That's why I accepted the transfer with my company. I really wasn't certain I could do anything on my own."* Gloria told a similar story of growing up with too much fertilizer. She compared it to having once killed a plant with too much plant food. It had looked unbelievably healthy for a few days, but then it turned yellow and died.

Entertaining: Casual To Candlelight

Clarke also spoke of his fertilizer, but it was a different brand. Clarke was an Orange whose ultra-Orange father had had numerous affairs before he left Clarke's mother when Clarke was in high school. No matter how successful he was in his work and in the community, Clarke suggested, he lived with the fear that he might be a ticking time bomb waiting to explode in some way like his father. Sally, who could not stress enough how caring Clarke had been throughout their marriage, told stories about her stable Green/Gold family that never understood her Blue sensitivity.

Both couples decided that there was a great deal they could learn from one another. Clarke and Sally wanted to develop the Gold aspects of their lives that Clarke had actually craved but feared – and Sally had avoided at every turn. Gloria and Dan wanted to learn how to let go and laugh. When Clarke asked Gloria and Dan what that would look like, Gloria said, "We would be able to go on a vacation with less than six suitcases and with at least one day where we had no plan whatsoever other than to relax."

Clarke and Sally suggested that they would love to develop an itinerary for a trip with Dan's help. Sally said, "It would be great to go on a vacation and not wonder what we had forgotten or whether or not we could find a motel room each night."

The couples decided to meet twice a month over the next six months to plan their vacation together – alternating dinner from one house to the other. Dan and Gloria were assigned the task of preparing a unique surprise for the group, and Clarke and Sally were assigned to develop the itinerary, knowing that on one of those days it would be scrapped to make way for the surprise. By the time they actually took their vacation (to Mexico) numerous friends and family members were as anxious to learn the results of this exercise as were the two couples.

The Green/Orange Clarke and Blue/Orange Sally forgot a bag, but they didn't need to worry since the Gold Dan and Gloria had extras of everything. Dan and Gloria's surprise excursion turned out to be very organized, but they had insisted that the guide choose their hotel. They all laughed about the difference in definitions of "hotel" from a U.S. city to a third world village.

Here were two couples that trusted one another enough to try some organic relationship building. Not only did they grow new skills, they came to appreciate their existing skills to a greater degree. Most importantly, they had fun growing their own relationship fruits and vegetables. And they found themselves entertaining other couples who wanted to try their hand at organic relationship building.

But a casual dinner is less stressful than a candlelight dinner. As we turn our attention to this formal occasion, ask yourself how circumstances change when you are trying to get someone's attention or to take a relationship to a more intimate level.

Dining by Candlelight

What do you do once you get to know someone and you want to take the relationship to the next level? Going back to Figure 6.1, you can see that this is a potentially high-risk, high-gain situation. You need (or at least think you need) this person, but you don't know whether or not they need you. Is there any wonder that such situations bring back every fear you ever had, why you feel that those adolescent pimples could reappear at any moment? What greater risk is there than telling someone that you need them without knowing whether or not they feel the same way?

What is the purpose of candlelight dining? Well for one thing, it masks spots on the glasses and wrinkles or blemishes on your face. It also makes it harder for the other person to see your flushed cheeks when some dish doesn't taste as good as you had hoped or when you think you asked the wrong question. And incidentally, if you play soft music in the background, it also muffles the pounding of your heart and your labored breathing.

Over twenty years ago Gerald Jampolsky (1979) suggested that individuals ask the following five questions as a means of retraining their minds to love by letting go of fear.

1. *Do I choose to experience **peace of mind** or do I choose to experience **conflict**?*

2. *Do I choose to experience **love** or **fear**?*

3. *Do I choose to be a **love finder** or a **fault finder**?*

4. *Do I choose to be a **love giver** or a **love seeker**?*

5. *Is this communication (verbal or non-verbal) loving to the other person and is it loving to me?*

Take a moment to think about these five questions. How could you use them in preparing for a candlelight dinner?

1. Do I choose to experience *peace of mind* or do I choose to experience *conflict*?

Life is not an experience that we can control. Planning is a good thing. Worry is not. As you prepare to invite someone to join you in taking a relationship to a more intimate level, ask yourself why you are attracted to this person and why he or she might be attracted to you. Figure 6.2 provides a format for you to use in answering these questions. You can use it to list the strengths and liabilities of your respective colors.

What We Bring to the Table
Figure 6.2

What I Bring to the Table		What My Partner Brings to the Table	
My Strengths	My Liabilities	Partner's Strengths	Partner's Liabilities

Entertaining: Casual To Candlelight

This chart helps you recognize several things. Notice that it begins with your strengths. You have something positive to offer to this relationship. Notice also that it ends with your partner's liabilities. Both you and your partner bring potential liabilities to the relationship. Both of you are human beings. You have the ability to set the tone or add to it, but neither can control it without the consent of the other. The question is whether you both want to take the relationship to the next level, not whether you could.

If you are Blue, don't allow your tendency to look at life as holistic to convince you that a rejection of your overture is a rejection of you. If you are Gold, don't allow your need to "measure up" to convince you that a rejection means that you didn't. If you are a Green, don't allow your normal skepticism to convince you that you don't even have a chance. And if you are Orange, don't allow your sense of adventure to turn this relationship into a contest. Intimacy doesn't have winners and losers.

2. Do I choose to experience *love* or *fear*?

Love is open and vulnerable. Fear is closed and guarded. You cannot enter into an honest relationship unless you are willing to make yourself vulnerable. If you hope for the best, you may be disappointed in the event that your love is rejected. If you worry about being rejected from the beginning, you may get what you expected. No matter what your Color, love is a Blue process. It is about holistic, emotional connections. You may need to proceed through a Gold logistical plan, through a Green sense of skepticism, or through an Orange sense of busying yourself before you can find your Blue. But make no mistake, love is Blue and it is built on hope and belief in the fundamental value of human beings – your own and others.

It's been said that when the Great Wallenda fell from the high wire to his death, a reporter asked his wife if she knew what was different about her husband's preparation that day. She supposedly replied, "Yes, he was worried about falling from the wire instead of focusing on walking it."

3. Do I choose to be a *love finder* or a *fault finder*?

If you choose to focus on love, the strengths that people bring to the table, you will see it. Conversely, if you choose to focus on people's liabilities, you will lose sight of their strengths. Greens and Golds are particularly susceptible to focusing on the things that don't measure up. Oranges and Blues are particularly susceptible to focusing on the things that do – Blues because they see what they want to see and Oranges because they sometimes see events without considering the conditions surrounding them.

You can recognize liabilities without dwelling on them. Don't forget Cicero's six mistakes. They get in people's way as much today as they did 2500 years ago.

Mistake #1	Thinking of life in terms of winners and losers
Mistake #2	Worrying about things over which you have little control
Mistake #3	Assuming that no answer exists because you don't know what it is

Mistake #4	Settling for what you know without considering what might be possible
Mistake #5	Failing to read and learn about new ideas
Mistake #6	Attempting to force others to believe and live as you do

4. Do I choose to be a *love giver* or a *love seeker*?

Both Victor Frankl (1959) and Mahaly Csikszentmihalyi (1990) warn us that we seldom find love by seeking it. Instead, it returns to us when we give it. You cannot give something you do not have to give. If you are confident without being arrogant and strong without being obnoxious, you can risk being vulnerable within a relationship. Love is the act of reaching out to make a connection with another human being. If you are not watching for opportunities to reach out for love, these opportunities will pass you by.

If you have trouble allowing yourself to be vulnerable, build a vulnerability plan for your day. Make a commitment to greet every person who walks toward you during the day. Simply say hello and ask them how their day is going. Also commit to starting a conversation with at least two strangers you meet. You can say something as simple as, "Wow, isn't this a noisy elevator." OR "Did you notice how windy it is out there today?" You will be surprised how many people will respond to your overture. These greetings probably won't help you find your soul-mate, but they will brighten your day and perhaps brighten someone else's day as well.

5. Is this communication *(verbal or non-verbal)* loving to the other person and is it loving to me?

Love is a connection with another human being. It often begins with a physical attraction or sometimes with an attraction to someone's wealth, position, or power. But it is seldom sustained by any of these. Remember that we said a relationship involves more than parallel play. If you enter a relationship with the idea of changing the other person, you will probably experience your own Pygmalion effect. You will risk destroying what it was that attracted you to that person in the first place. On the other hand, if you enter into a relationship with the idea that you will change to make the other person happy, you will probably disappoint both that person and yourself.

Relationships require a balance. Think about what you and your partner bring to the table. Build on those strengths to explore other aspects of your mutual rainbow. Work hard to ensure that neither of you loses your identity among your combined Colors. Organic relationships last long after the candles from your first intimate dinner burnout. But don't forget to plan candlelight dinners periodically throughout your relationship. They remind you of the common purpose that first set you on your course together.

Summary

What you are as a member in a relationship is a result of who you are as a person – your strengths and your liabilities. Do you know what you and

Entertaining: Casual To Candlelight

your various relationship partners bring to the table? Have you learned various recipes for understanding what motivates you as well as what motivates other people. Have you used enough cookbooks to have learned what you like and to have gained the confidence to create your own recipes? Have you washed off the residue from past pesticides and fertilizers so that you focus on your own and other people's strengths?

If so, you may be ready to experiment with growing your own relationship food. Go ahead; give it a try. It is the most natural experience you can have.

Getting Ready To Entertain

1. Use Csikszentmihalyi's recipe (1990) to plan how you and a partner might take a friendship to a new level.

   a. *Choose a challenging relationship task that you have a chance of completing.*

   b. *How will you concentrate on growing these relationship skills?*

   c. *What are your goals for this task?*

   d. *How will you and your partner provide feedback to one another?*

   e. *How and when will you practice on something that is not a part of your daily responsibilities?*

   f. *What obstacles do you have for controlling your own actions, and how will you overcome them?*

   g. *How will you work to let go of self-conscious fears that may prevent you from reaching a higher level of consciousness?*

   h. *When will you set aside time for practice?*

2. Use Jampolsky's recipe (1979) to retrain your mind to love by letting go of fear.

   a. *How do you choose to experience peace of mind rather than experiencing conflict?*

   b. *Describe how you choose to experience love rather than fear?*

   c. *In what ways are you a love finder rather than a fault finder?*

   d. *List several ways in which you have chosen to be a love giver rather than a love seeker?*

   e. *What evidence do you have that you have made your verbal and non-verbal communications loving to your relationship partner and to yourself?*

3. What other readings and exercises do you plan to undertake in order to build your relationship skills?

References

Covey, S. (1989). *The seven habits of highly effective people: Restoring the character ethic.* New York: Simon & Schuster.

Csikszentmihalyi, M. (1990). *Flow.* New York: Harper & Row.

Frankl, V. (1959). *Man's search for meaning: An introduction to logotherapy.* New York: Simon and Schuster.

Gardner, H. (1993). *Multiple intelligences: The theory in practice.* New York: Basic Books.

Goleman, D. (1995). *Emotional intelligence: Why it can matter more than I.Q.* New York: Bantam Books.

Hart, L. (1983). *Human brain, human learning.* New York: Longman.

Jampolsky. G. (1979). *Love is letting go of fear.* Berkeley, CA: Celestial Arts.

References

Johnson, D. (2005). *Sustaining change in schools: How to overcome differences and focus on quality.* Alexandria, VA: Association for Supervision and Curriculum Development.

Johnson, D. (2004) *The Real Colors Homeowner's Guide: A follow-up to your Real Colors Workshop.* Phoenix, AZ: National Curriculum & Training Institute, Inc.

Keirsey, D. and Bates, M. (1998). *Please understand me II: Temperament, character, intelligence.* Del Mar, CA: Prometheus Nemesis Books.

Montgomery, S. (1989). *The Pygmalion project: Love and coercion among types.* DelMar, CA: Prometheus Nemesis Books.

Montgomery, S. (2002). *People Patterns: A modern guide to the four temperaments.* DelMar, CA: Prometheus Nemesis Books.

Nelson, W. (1994). *"There are worse things than being alone."* New York: Liberty Records.

Piaget, J. (1952). *The origins of intelligence in the child.* New York: International Universities Press.

Quinn, R. (1996). *Deep change.* San Francisco: Jossey-Bass.

Wason, B. (1970) *The everything cookbook.* New York: Hawthorn Books, Inc.

Conclusion

You can have Real relationships in your life. You can feel comfortable enough with another person to invite them into your home, to ask them to share your table, to share conversation, and to explore one another's hopes and dreams. Opening yourself to this type of personal connection carries

Conclusion

with it both opportunities and obstacles. It takes a willingness to risk, to develop enough trust with another person that you can share the personal details that can only be shared from inside your Color home.

What do you bring to the table — your personality "stuff?" What does your relationship partner bring to the table? Your Color "stuff" can either promote or impede your own personal growth. It can also promote or impede your relationships with other people. You can share your personality stuff with other human beings and appreciate their stuff. You can learn how to promote and sustain a positive balance between your stuff and their stuff — to monitor and grow a personal relationship. You can then use Real Colors to create a positive attitude toward others and toward life in general. By learning to manage your environment rather than your relationships, you can explore the nuances of relationships within various stages of intimacy.

There are no magic bullets for ensuring meaningful and lasting relationships. But there are numerous lenses through which you can develop a clearer picture of potentially positive relationships in the world around you. Real Colors provides such a lens. How willing are you to analyze the fertilizer and pesticide residues that cloud your picture of the world? How willing are you to grow meaningful relationships with other people. They don't just happen magically. You create and nurture them.

What are you waiting for? Relationships can sometimes be painful and difficult to maintain. But the alternative to meaningful relationships is loneliness. You have more to offer other people than you might realize. There is no time like the present. Why not start today?